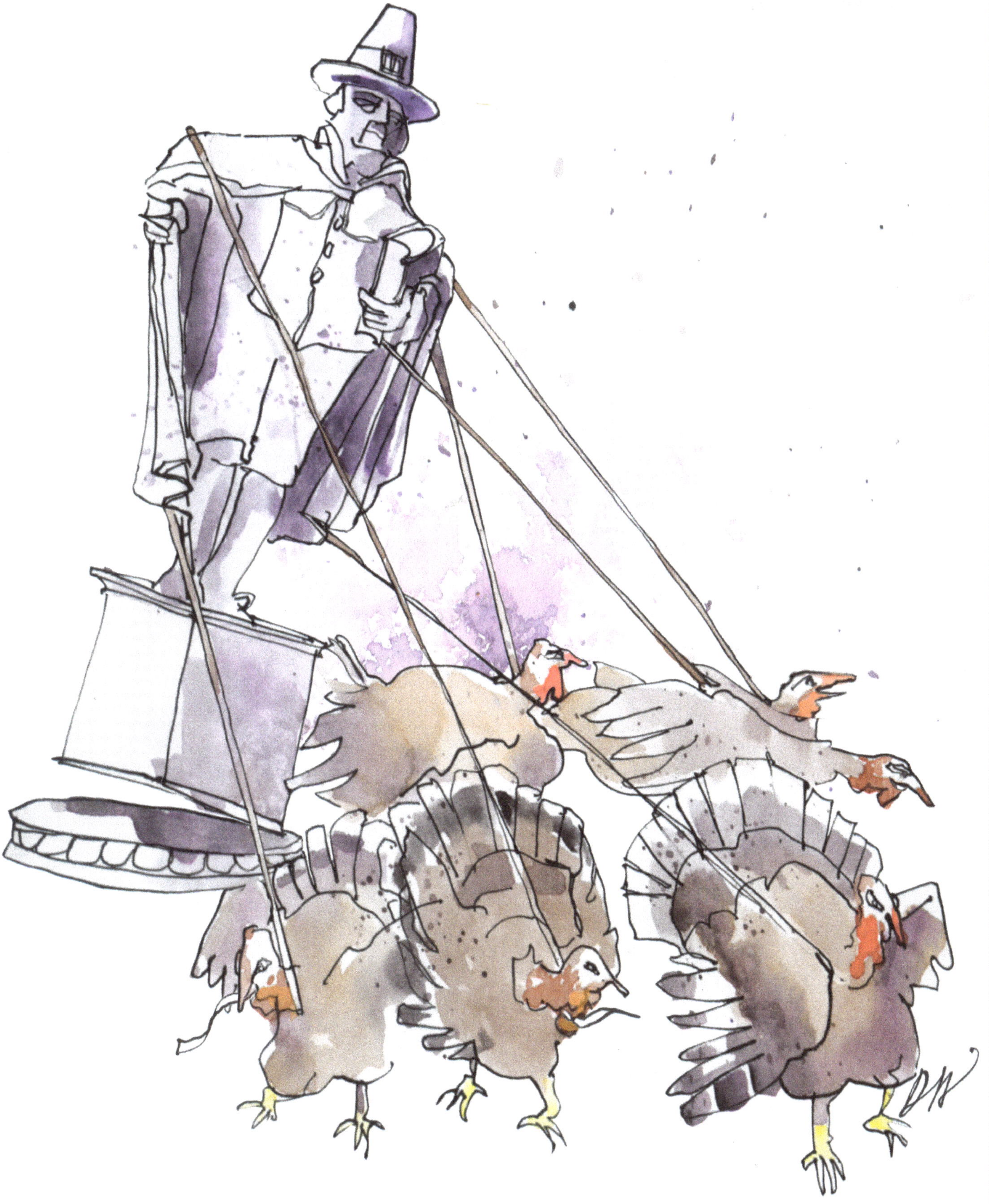

PUBLISHER'S LETTER
BY MICHAEL GERBER & ALAN GOLDBERG

IN PRAISE OF BRIAN

*How best to celebrate **Bystander's** fifth anniversary? By celebrating the man who made it all possible.*

Thirty years ago, I was a bright, splendidly educated, viscerally optimistic 21-year-old ready to foist myself on an unsuspecting world. Everything—from the thickness of my hair, to the CIA recruiters slipping flyers under my door, to the naked woman smushed up next to me—augured a future of preposterous abundance. So: what next? Where to spend my one and only life? Historian, or diplomat? Senator? Spy? Where did the world need me most?

Looking back today—in the time of COVID, after an election that's felt like the tailgate before a Civil War—I feel pretty goddamn dumb. I think, "If I were a lawyer, I could help with the ballots. If I were a doctor, I could help with the vaccine. If I were a spy, I could help Putin's dick fall off." But instead? Jokes. On Twitter. A whole generation of the so-called best and brightest fell for the same self-swindle. If the American Century is over, one epitaph might be, "Sorry everybody—the money was better at *Saturday Night Live*."

If that's one type of comedy writer, Brian McConnachie is the other: the type who owes no apology. Whatever profession he picked, Brian's incomparable whimsy would've forced itself to the surface. I've been told he worked in advertising, but that's like saying Superman worked in journalism. He was biding his time, laying in wait, waiting to assume his final form.

To give you an idea of what I mean: every Thursday we have a *Bystander* partner call. Last week it began somberly, because Brian had a minor medical procedure. Alan and I did the sympathetic friend thing, because: hospital. Seventies. COVID.

Brian put up with that for about four seconds. "Thanks guys, I'm fine. Hey, I just thought of a new idea for a cartoon." (See below.) Even semi-conscious, The McConnachie makes us laugh as naturally and inevitably as The Macallan gets us drunk. One doesn't edit him, one just adds a little water or, if you're really smart, nothing at all. Because Brian McConnachie was *born* to be a comedy writer, and that he found his way to *Lampoon*, to *SNL*, to *SCTV*, to NPR, to here, is one of the few things that gives me genuine faith. It is, as Franklin said, "proof that God loves us and wants us to be happy."

People like Brian must be nurtured, encouraged, protected like a natural resource. They are part of our Strategic National Reserve. If Midwestern families don't trek out twelve hours both ways to have their pictures taken in front of him, as he spurts out something hilarious every seven-and-a-half minutes, they should. And we should celebrate him all the more for doing it anyway. If I made the right decision thirty years ago, Brian, you're the reason why. We made this for you.—*MG*

Brian and I met about 45 years ago when he came to the New York public TV station where I was a writer and producer. He was already Brian McConnachie, ex-*National Lampoon* editor, *SNL* and *SCTV* writer, Woody Allen film actor, *etc. etc.* He came in with wonderful ideas—the Upper East Side reworking of an opera, *Porter and Beth*; the how-to book *So You Found a Squirrel*. I was thrilled to be able to work with him, bringing his pieces to air, and then, in the radio studio, taking part in some of them. They were all very funny and unexpected rearrangements of the known world. Brian never worked outside the box. For Brian, there is no box.

And being Brian, it was always a joint effort. We became close friends in no small part because of how much he wants to share what he loves, a kindness that defines him. To be honest, we share a certain lack of self-certainty, which makes figuring things out that much more fun. Even with non-comic projects we could do together, like rebuilding a gazebo in his backyard, we could pretend to be so wise, while knowing how little we actually knew.

Hanging with Brian, maybe riding in a car with him, listening to Gershwin or Porter or Hart on a CD, and watching the era recaptured in his delight, is one of life's great pleasures.

There were years before we had the luck to meet Michael, trying to get our radio serial heard. And there were always people willing to help. Brian was and is the center of a fairy tale about a happy little band. Everyone wants to support Brian, because everyone gets to see the world a bit differently just by knowing him.

Enjoy this issue, and feel, as we all do, a happy band member.—*AG*

Harry Bliss & Steve Martin

THE PERFECT HOLIDAY GIFT FOR ANYONE (OR EVERYONE!) ON YOUR LIST

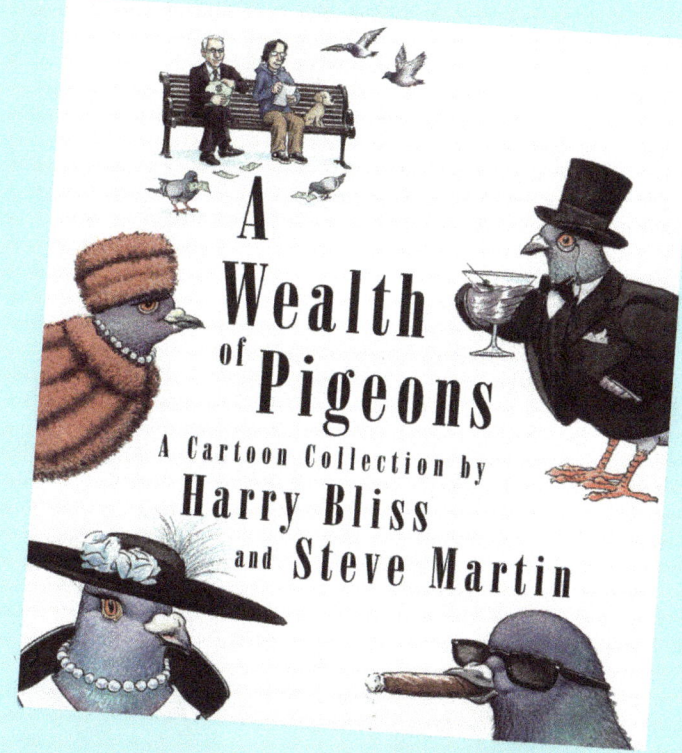

A WEALTH OF PIGEONS

A Cartoon Collection by acclaimed *New Yorker* cartoonist Harry Bliss and multi-talented comedian Steve Martin

ON SALE
NOVEMBER 17
AVAILABLE EVERYWHERE BOOKS ARE SOLD

TABLE OF CONTENTS

Brian McConnachie in his office at The National Lampoon, *1974.*

DEPARTMENTS
Frontispiece: "Turkey Day" **by D. Watson**..............................1
Publisher's Letter **by Michael Gerber & Alan Goldberg**......2
Last Look?: "Donald Trump" **by Zoe Matthiessen**..............76

GALLIMAUFRY
Brian McConnachie, Charles Barsotti, Nick Spooner, Rich Sparks, Ivan Ehlers, John Jonik, Lance Hansen...................11

SHORT STUFF
Spotlight **by Ellis Rosen**...8
Who Am I? **by Brian McConnachie**..19
The Ding Dong Hoodlum Priest **by Brian McConnachie**......20
A Letter to the Commish **by Brian McConnachie**................22
Inspirational Animal Stories #1: The Motivational Tiger
    by Brian McConnachie...24
Connie and the Fifth Time **by Brian McConnachie**..............26
Johnny Bullwhip **by Brian McConnachie**.............................28

FEATURES
Wigglesworth **by Brian McConnachie**..................................31
McConnachie to Brown **by Brian McConnachie**..................36
The Dracula Letters
    by Jack Handey and Brian McConnachie......................38
Hi Brian! **by Ed Subitzky**...43
The Birth of the Bystander **by Shary Flenniken**..............44

The AMERICAN BYSTANDER

Founded 1981 by Brian McConnachie
#17 • Vol. 5, No. 1 • October 2020

EDITOR & PUBLISHER
Michael Gerber
HEAD WRITER Brian McConnachie
SENIOR EDITOR Alan Goldberg
ORACLE Steve Young
STAFF LIAR P.S. Mueller
INTREPID TRAVELER Mike Reiss
EAGLE EYES Patrick L. Kennedy
AGENTS OF THE SECOND BYSTANDER INTERNATIONAL
Eve Alintuck, Joey Green, Matt Kowalick, Neil Mitchell, Maxwell Ziegler
MANAGING EDITOR EMERITA
Jennifer Finney Boylan
WARTIME CONSIGLIERA
Kate Powers
CONTRIBUTORS
Charles Barsotti, Louisa Bertman, Barry Blitt, Chris Bonno, George Booth, Ella Bracy, Mike Bracy, Andy Breckman, M.K. Brown, Roz Chast, T.Q. Chen, Joe Ciardiello, Bob Eckstein, Ivan Ehlers, Sam Evans, Shary Flenniken, E.R. Flynn, Rick Geary, Phoebe Geer, Michael Gold, Sam Gross, Orrin Grossman, Jack Handey, Lance Hansen, Brandon Hicks, Tim Hunt, John Jonik, Victor Juhasz, Chris Kelly, Sean Kelly, Lars Kenseth, Paul Kleba, Stephen Kroninger, Rob Mariani, Zoe Matthiessen, Deborah McManus, Rick Meyerowitz, Lawrence Murphy, Mary O'Hara, Timothy O'Hara, David Ostow, Dennis Perrin, Nathan Place, Jonathan Plotkin, Ellis Rosen, Dan Salomon, Mike Shiell, Art Silverman, Rich Sparks, Frank Springer, Nick Spooner, Ed Subitzky, Dave Thomas, B.A. Van Sise, B.K. Taylor, Dalton Vaughn, D. Watson, Bill Woodman, Nathan Yoder, and Jack Ziegler.

Mary & Ann McConnachie, Andrew Alexander, Bob Bloomberg, Lanky Bareikis, Karen Backus, Alleen Schultz,, Joe Lopez, Ivanhoe & Gumenick, Greg & Trish, *et al.*
NAMEPLATES BY Mark Simonson
ISSUE CREATED BY Michael Gerber

Vol. 5, No. 1. ©2020 Good Cheer LLC, all rights reserved. Proudly produced in sunny Santa Monica, California, USA.

"BOYLAN'S WRY WIT, WICKED SENSE OF HUMOR, AND UNIQUE WAY OF TURNING PHRASES SHINE THROUGH…"
~KIRKUS REVIEWS

GOOD BOY
MY LIFE IN SEVEN DOGS

A NEW MEMOIR BY JENNIFER FINNEY BOYLAN, *NEW YORK TIMES* BESTSELLING AUTHOR OF *SHE'S NOT THERE: A LIFE IN TWO GENDERS*

"*Good Boy* is a warm, funny, instantly engaging testament to the power of love—canine and human—to ease us through life's radical transitions. And I say that as a cat person!"

~JENNIFER EGAN
Winner of the Pulitzer Prize and author of *A Visit from the Goon Squad* and *Manhattan Beach*

"Dogs help us understand ourselves: who we are, who we've been. They teach us what it means to love, and to be loved. They bear witness to our joys and sorrows; they lick the tears from our faces. And when our backs are turned, they steal a whole roasted chicken off the supper table."

~JENNIFER FINNEY BOYLAN

ON SALE APRIL 21, 2020 — PRE-ORDER NOW

CELADONBOOKS.COM/BOOKSHOP

Baseball Is Hunting *by Brian McConnachie*..........................45
Cowboys on a Walnut Farm *by Brian McConnachie*............56
Life Of Brian
 by Jack Handey, Lawrence Murphy, Rob Mariani, Mike Bracy, Jack Ziegler, Bill Woodman, Rick Meyerowitz, Mary O'Hara, Ella Bracy, Dave Thomas, Phoebe Geer, Jenny Boylan, Art Silverman, Timothy O'Hara, Sam Evans, Chris Kelly, Orrin Grossman, Dennis Perrin, Sean Kelly and Deborah McManus 62

OUR BACK PAGES
Notes From a Small Planet *by Rick Geary* 73
The Kroninger Collection *by Stephen Kroninger*.................75

CARTOONS, PHOTOS & ILLUSTRATIONS BY
Victor Juhasz, Dalton Vaughn, Michael Gold, George Booth, Barry Blitt, Sam Gross, Ellis Rosen, Charles Barsotti, Nick Spooner, Rich Sparks, Ivan Ehlers, John Jonik, Lance Hansen, Jonathan Plotkin, Chris Bonno, Louisa Bertman, Nathan Yoder, T.Q. Chen, Tim Hunt, Brandon Hicks, B.K. Taylor, David Ostow and Dan Salomon, Paul Kleba, Ed Subitzky, Shary Flenniken, Andy Breckman, Bob Eckstein, Mike Shiell, E.R. Flynn, Nathan Place, Joe Ciardiello, Lars Kenseth, B.A. Van Sise, Bill Woodman, Frank Springer, Roz Chast, Rick Geary, Stephen Kroninger, and Zoe Matthiessen.

............◆............

Sam's Spot

COVER

Leave it to the incomparable artist/alchemist **VICTOR JUHASZ** to make something great out of our ongoing environmental castastrophe. We are happy to report that full breaths are back on the menu here at *Bystander* HQ, something definitely not the case for about a month. The kids playing in the pile of ash? Future *Bystander* readers…and/or contributors.

ACKNOWLEDGMENTS

All material is ©2020 its creators, all rights reserved; please do not reproduce/distribute it without written consent of the creators and *Bystander*. Several items originally appeared in Rick Meyerowitz's excellent history of *The National Lampoon* magazine, *Drunk Stoned Brilliant Dead*: Michael Gold's photograph of Brian on page 4; Rick's memories of Brian on page 65-66, and Chris Kelly's ecomium on page 70-71. Thanks to Rick for permission to reprint this material, now go read his book. The screenshot from SCTV is ©1981 The Second City, and is used with permission.

THE AMERICAN BYSTANDER, *Vol. 5, No. 1*, (978-0-578-77386-5). Publishes ~5x/year. ©2020 by Good Cheer LLC. No part of this magazine can be reproduced, in whole or in part, by any means, without the written permission of the Publisher. For this and other queries, email *Publisher@ americanbystander.org*, or write: Michael Gerber, Publisher, *The American Bystander*, 1122 Sixth St., #403, Santa Monica, CA 90403. **Subscribe at www.patreon.com/bystander.** Other info can be found at www.americanbystander.org.

EARIOS

THE MARGARET CHO

ICONIC COMEDIAN MARGARET CHO TALKS WITH PEOPLE YOU KNOW, AND PEOPLE YOU SHOULD KNOW.

  acast

SIX OF THE BEST
BY ELLIS ROSEN
SPOTLIGHT
A few cartoons beyond all mortal sanity

PANDORA'S JUNK DRAWER

"Don't tell the Great Leader, Master of All That Is Known, He Who Shall Bring Us To Utopia, that I'm just in this cult ironically."

"Does this hat say 'cosmic terror beyond all mortal sanity'?"

"Sure, he's Gregor Samsa now..."

"Who's the artist?"

"Honey, look—those are the tiles I was thinking about for the kitchen."

ELLIS ROSEN (@EllisRosen) *is a cartoonist living in Brooklyn. He's appeared in* **The New Yorker** *and many other places; read his weekly cartoon series, Junk Drawer, at GoComics.com.*

Elvis is Alive and Well
inside these pages

Seymour Chwast
Steven Brower

The Mighty ELVIS
A Graphic Biography

Seymour Chwast
Steven Brower

Contents

- Introduction
- In the Beginning
- Sun Records
- Musical Influences
- First Records
- Col. Parker
- Jackie Gleason
- Milton Berle
- Ed Sullivan
- In the Army
- Graceland
- Viva Las Vegas
- Frank Sinatra
- Concerts
- Pink Cadillac
- Poster
- Women (and One Man) Who Dated Elvis
- Masculine Idols / Heroes
- Films
- Comeback
- The Beatles
- Elvis Meets Nixon
- What He Wore
- Hair
- Guitars
- Songs
- Tours
- Priscilla
- Divorce / Drugs
- Final Days
- Filmography
- Albums
- Singles
- The Critics
- Elvis Speaks
- What He Ate
- Bibliography

www.yoebooks.com

STAFF
Gallimaufry

For over a decade, Brian wrote and performed pieces for NPR. Here are a few of his best.

THIS I BELIEVE.

Before I begin with what I believe, I feel compelled to say I believe that the "This" should probably go after the "I Believe" and not precede it. It makes it sound a bit arcane in origin. It makes it sound a bit 1950s Biblical rewrite. Or we could lose the this entirely. No one's going to be wondering what's being believed here. It's redundant. It's pretentious. It's cleaner without it. I also believe that if I keep going on about this, some of the more strident and doctrinaire as staff members from NPR will start plotting to drag me off to some soundproof room in the middle of the night and bring me to my senses. But enough about the this.

What I believe, what I really know, is that if you're ever waiting in a closet to jump out and scare someone, that day for some reason that person is never going to open that closet door and you're just going to be stuck in there with all the wool coats wondering why in heaven's name you believed this was a good idea to begin with.

However, I also believe that if you stay in that closet long enough, beyond any reasonable amount of time, when that person eventually does open the closet, he or she will get the scare of their life, major fright, hysterical screaming—so loud in fact that you really might want to rethink this whole jumping out of closets at people. And that is what I believe most of the time, usually. And then a day will come along and wham, I won't believe a word of it. I find life is like that.

And unless your beliefs are limited to universals like where North is—and even that gets relative—you had better prepare yourself, if you're even vaguely open-minded, for radical confusion, where in time every notion you've ever believed will be legitimately stood on its head. So if you're still serious about hiding in the closet to scare people, that's fine. I'm not here to judge you. What can I tell you? Be patient. Stay quiet. Bring something to read. A little flashlight, bring a sandwich. And don't forget to listen.

You want to be ready with your special scary face when that door finally opens. What you might want to do to give this act some meaning is imagine the person who is about to open the door represents reality coming to the closet of—we'll call the closet what closets have always been—our triumph over chaos. And reality has come to our triumph over chaos to put on the overcoat of common belief.

And the very last thing reality expects is you, and this is you as you—you get to play you, the everyman, a little guy—leaping out and scaring the living daylights out of it. But that's exactly what it needs. Reality has played pretty fast and loose with us over the years and it has never once been held accountable. So cosmically I like what you're doing here. I think you are really on to something. And I hope that this has been a part of the puzzle that you have been looking for. And that we eventually rename this segment the "That For Which In Vain We Have So Plaintively Been Looking For," or something equally as catchy. And I thank you for listening. *(April 6, 2007)*

FIGHTING ATOP A MOVING TRAIN.

The next time you see someone climbing up on the roof of a moving train and chasing after whoever else may be up there and engaging them in a fist fight, you might ask yourself—isn't that dangerous?

You'd think they go into the parlor car to slug it out, unless it was the people in the parlor car who told the brawlers to take it outside and up a flight. But say you find yourself in this situation. There are some things to consider while you're up there, such as if your back is facing the direction that the train is traveling in. You have to rely on the person you're in the fistfight with to warn you—hey, tunnel coming up, better duck—and then realize: can you really trust the person you're fighting with to warn you about low tunnels, or is this the railroad equivalent of—hey, look, your shoe's untied? A low-clearance tunnel victory is an ugly way to win a train

"I'm O.K., Al, it's just Trump fatigue."

GENDER REVEAL PARTY

TA-DAAAH!

SPOONER

top fight, but for some guys it's all they have. What about hats, you might ask. Say you decided to wear a hat that day, and good for you. More and more people are wearing hats. Hats are nice. Hats are good, but they're absolutely worthless in a fist-fight on top of a speeding train. You're not going to land too many punches lying on your stomach in the dark of a tunnel clinging to the roof of a train and pulling your hat down tight over your ears with one hand and throwing punches into the dark with the other. Then—uh-oh—your pants start to come undone. While trying to fix the problem with your pants, guess what? Your hat blows off and then you want to go chasing after it. I know. It's instinctual. But forget the hat. It's gone. You can buy another one. Try and concentrate on this fight you've gotten yourself into. But who was doing all this train-top fighting, you might ask. Well, cowboys who refuse to admit their train-roof fighting days are over, spies, of course, acrobatic hobos, train robbers, people who can't find their seats, people who can find their seats but other people are in them —the list goes on and on. What are they actually fighting about and is it worth it? Lately, some hot-button issues have included how much do our souls weigh and are elephants the only mammals that have four knees? On the other hand, what about putting a stop to this brawl? Say you're in a sleeping car in an upper bunk in your pajamas trying to read the latest copy of AARP and you hear all this thumping and banging around on the roof of the train. And you think that's it, I'm going to put a stop to this. I can't say I like your odds, but you might consider before you enter into the fray with whoever else is up there, is my hat on tight enough? And you'd better retie the pull string on your pajama bottoms. These have been some thoughts to ponder the next time you see men chasing each other around on the roof of a speeding train and thinking, hey, that looks like fun. Well, it isn't, and I hope these thoughts have been helpful to you. *(December 11, 2015)*

WELCOME TO THE WORLD, SAMANTHA.

Our neighbors just had a baby girl, Samantha. Welcome to the land of the free and the home of the brave, Samantha. As you grow and your eyes focus, I'd like to point out a few things you might like about being a Yank.

One thing you'll probably notice are all those bottles and such under the sink. Consider their names for a moment. Cheer. Joy. Behold. Dawn. Bounty. Fantastik. Mop 'n' Glo. Fab. Are they not the cleaning products of a happy people? It almost makes you want to start scrubbing floors.

Then, before you know it, Samantha, you'll be tying your own shoes. Do you know that the strongest shoelaces in the world are made right here in the U.S.? That's why the authorities take them away when they put you behind bars.

We are also a sports-loving people, with a penchant for poetry. As in, "Getting a fastball by Henry Aaron was like getting a sunrise past a rooster." Pretty good, huh?

As you keep growing, you're going to have heroes who reflect the talent of the American character. Some of mine are E.B. White, Willie Mays, George Gershwin and Martha Stewart.

You might then reply, "But gee, Mr. Mac, we just learned in Social Studies *and* Home Ec, she's a convicted felon."

Be that as it may, I include Martha Stewart because of her mashed potatoes. I am absolutely convinced that if she had given the judge a bowl of her fabulous mashed potatoes, that judge would've yelled out, "Case dismissed!" found a spoon, and retired to chambers. Her mashed potatoes are just that good.

But she didn't take the easy way out. She didn't play the mashed potato card. And she didn't whine. She sucked it up, handed over her shoelaces, and did her stretch. And we are only left to imagine what she could've created with a pair of American shoelaces and that much time to kill.

And speaking of mashed potatoes, Samantha, we are also a musical people who love to dance. You'll probably begin with the Chicken Dance, the Bunny Hop and the Hokey Pokey, and then move on to the more interpretive styles of the Watusi, the Frug and the Bump, followed by the cha-cha, twist and tango, then waltzing your way to the "Macarena," on through the Mashed Potato and the Lambada, the forbidden dance of love, all the way on to hot dance disco.

Hopefully stopping along the way for another pop favorite, the bossa nova. Which I am quick to add is the only dance which takes complete responsibility for itself. Its own lyrics declare, "Blame it on the bossa nova." You're not going to find that happening in Herzegovina.

And somewhere around the age of thirty, you should definitely know what you want to do with your life. The Pentagon looks dysfunctional; maybe you can help out there.

So let's review: Happy cleaning products equal a happy people. American shoelaces—ask if you can hold on to yours. Hey, you never know. De Tocqueville—now, there was no mention of de Tocqueville, but when dealing with the sociology of a people, it's always good to mention de Tocqueville. What about mashed potatoes? Well, eat them in moderation. But never with a spoon, it looks prehensile. And we never eat them while dancing.

So, Samantha, in conclusion, as Lincoln said to de Tocqueville, most people are as happy as they want to be. But to paraphrase Dorothy, if you can't find happiness under your own kitchen sink, maybe you should check under the bathroom sink. But if it isn't there, you know what, blame it on the bossa nova. *(December 27, 2010)*

AN ARGUMENT FOR DUMB DESIGN.

If intelligent design really wants equal billing, it might want to address a short list of grievances that include: head lice, ticks and mole rats, vultures and typhoons, migraines, earthquakes and tornadoes, crab apples, poison mushrooms, killer bees, fire ants, harelip and poison ivy, quicksand, hurricanes and termites, black holes in the universe, spiders that lay their eggs in the brains of other spiders, plantar warts and gangrene, vampire bats, wisdom teeth and frostbite, sinus pain, pederasty, incest and the hiccups, abstract expressionism, particle physics and AstroTurf, gnats, the Colonel's chicken, non-alcoholic beer, FEMA and hammertoes, varicose veins and pinworms, splinters—now strictly speaking, splinters should not qualify, but, I don't know, I just kinda threw it in there because life's tough enough and then you gotta worry about splinters--restless leg syndrome—Why not?—hammerhead sharks—for crazy design--floods and plagues and earwigs, poison sumac—whatever that is—Arctic cold fronts, torture and genocide, Super Bowl halftime, herpes, gonorrhea, syphilis and AIDS, nightmares, cramps and vomit, Republicans, bedbugs and Democrats, and—Wouldn't you know?—no unicorns. *(November 28, 2005)*

REDUPLICATIVES.

Stuck in a traffic jam, I noticed people don't call each other nincompoops anymore. And considering what we do call each other, nincompoop sounded pretty elegant. Then I sort of tumbled down a rabbit hole of rhythmic sounds I hadn't heard in a while, like fuddy-duddy, dillydally, Piggly Wiggly, Walla Walla, wickywacky, funny bunny, howdy doody, "Hokey Pokey," whoopsie daisy, loosey-goosey, Lackawanna, mamma mia, higgledy-piggledy, willy-nilly, Boola Boola, Tricky Dicky, ticky-tacky, Betsy Wetsy, Cancun, Lorna Doon, hubba-hubba, lucky ducky, Santa Ana, Ouagadougou, candelabra, hacky sacky, knickknack, Silly Billy, Wagga Wagga, tutti-frutti, cruncha cruncha, Benihana, chunky monkey, hully gully, "Hokey Pokey," Honolulu, Steady Eddie, ipso facto, hunky-dory, Polly wolly, Harry Caray, ipse dixit, Shuga Wuga, Luca Brasi—Luca Brasi?

Roly-poly, Ashtebula, Halle Berry, motor scooter, Handy Andy, golden oldie, Lille Langtry, calla lily, Nagasaki, freaky deaky, Catalina, Kitty Kelley, holy moly, Lana Turner, Ling-Ling, Scooby Dooby, Tamiami, Willy Wonka, Andy Panda, kumquat, kowtow, couscous, Corpus Christi, Fannie Farmer, oogabooga, helter skelter, teeter-totter, Peterborough, Pango Pango, Boutros Boutros-Ghali, Weehawken, topsy-turvy, cuckoo clock and, again, nincompoop. Thank you, and bye-bye. *(May 12, 2005)*

VETTING A POET LAUREATE.

Chairman of the Committee: Before we start, I'd just like the record to reflect the innumerable times I've heard my Congressional colleagues mutter, "Poetry lifts the veil from the hidden beauty of the world." We'll begin the questioning with Congressman Capshaw.

Capshaw: Thank you, Mr. Chairman. Mr. Lattner, would you tell this com-

LEGENDS OF ROCK

by Rich Sparks

mittee what you did before you became a poet?
Lattner: I was a guard at a, uh, closed truck weighing station, making sure that the trucks didn't break in and weigh themselves.
Capshaw: What have you been told about the position of Poet Laureate?
Lattner: I was told that the pay was $5.75 an hour, and I'd have to show all my poems to Mrs. Cheney.
Capshaw: Have any of the Federal agencies approached you to write poems for them? Like, the CIA or the FBI?
Lattner: The NRA has, yes.
Capshaw: The NRA's not a Federal agency.
Chairman: I don't think it is…
Lattner: They told me they were, and they had badges and paystubs.
Capshaw: What did they want you to write about?
Lattner: They wanted a poem about automatic assault weapons being misunderstood.
Capshaw: Tell us what you like writing about.
Lattner: I used to like writing about trees, until I read Joyce Kilmer and saw he pretty much closed the book on the subject. Now I like going to the beach with my St. Bernard and watching the seagulls. In fact, I brought one of my seagull poems with me. It's called, "A Seagull Named Freedom." Would you like to hear it?
Capshaw: No! Thank you…I'm trying to remember that woman poet's name—Edna St. Something. I want to say Edna St. Louis Missouri…
Chairman: Edna St. Paul Minnesota?
Capshaw: She wrote about candles burning at both ends…what is it?
Lattner: I know who you mean. It's like Edna St. Vincent DePaul.
Chairman: Edna St. Vincent Price?
Capshaw: Well, she wrote wonderful poems. They made sense, and they rhymed, and I'd like to test you if I may. If I were to say to you, "April is the cruelest month," quick now, make up the next line! What would you say?
Lattner: Well, "month" is what we call a hard rhyme. So I'd invert the first line—it's sort of a professional trick—but I'd start, *"The month that we call April is really very cruel/With rain as thick and heavy as a big dog's drool."* That's just off the top of my head.
Capshaw: That's both true and it rhymes! Mr. Chairman, I have no objection to this man becoming our Poet Laureate.
Chairman: So noted. Why don't we call a recess and resume in 15 minutes? **(September 20, 2004)**

OUR TOWN.
This is Brian McConnachie, and I'm here in Grover's Corners, New Hampshire, the town better known as "Our Town," the actual setting of the Thornton Wilder play of the same name.
[*A cow can be heard lowing.*]
We're here to witness something quite extraordinary. In an event that's been pretty exclusive to Pamplona, Spain, they're going to release an entire herd of bulls at the top of Main Street. This is intended, I gather, to give Grover's Corners a leg up in the tourist business.
The air here is really charged. And I have to mention: they've gathered some big, angry-looking bulls. So any moment now, we're going to have the first annual Running of the Bulls in Grover's Corners, New Hampshire.
[*A gate creaks open, followed by the sound of hoofs.*]
And here they come, right down Main Street. They are big fellas—
[*Someone groans in pain, followed by loud hoofbeats.*]
Woah! There goes the Stage Manager—he really took a header!
[*Sound of soft tissue impact.*]
Oh, that's not a place you want to get gored! That was Doc Gibbs, I think. He went straight up in the air, that's gonna hurt tomorrow!
Oh look! Emily Webb just showed up. I don't think she was expecting this!
[*A female groan.*]
…and she's down. This was definitely not a good day for her to come back from the beyond! She really got her ticket punched.
And there they go! It's not a very big Main Street they have here—the handlers are rounding up the bulls…this has been Brian McConnachie reporting from the first annual Running of the Bulls in Grover's Corners, New Hampshire. **(March 29, 2002)**

GET OUTSIDE THE BOX.
If we ever hope to get this great nation back into terrific shape, we have to take our hearts off our sleeve, put on our game face, and start thinking outside of the box.

We know the answers are out there, and it's up to each of us to go out there and bring some back.

Let's start with a hypothetical. Let's say the Defense Department won't talk

"Dammit! Did everybody here drink my invisibility potion?"

to the State Department. Let's take it outside the box and see what we come up with.

Ooookay, I'm leaving the box...

[Sound of creaky door opening, then shutting solidly. BRIAN'S VOICE is now echo-y, like he's floating in space]

I'm outside the box. I'm thinking outside the box...I'm totally receptive to everything...

Wooow. The first thing you notice is how many kinds of boxes there are to be out of.

I remember my mother had hatboxes. You don't see hatboxes anymore. Women don't wear big hats. The Queen of England does.

Okay, we're drifting here.

Now I'm thinking of the Boxer Rebellion. That got ugly in a hurry, didn't it? What was the main cause of the Boxer Rebellion? Was it a) a rebellion by rickshaw drivers who wanted to wear briefs, but the government said, "No! You wear boxers!" But they said, "But we can run faster in briefs!" so they took up arms. Or, b) professional boxers wanting to get paid upfront. Some of them wanted to get paid even in between rounds.

Why am I outside the box? Oh, the government people who won't talk to each other.

Whoa. I just had a thought: what if an angel floated by, and you grabbed it by the ankle. And for reasons only you could answer, you took a big bite out of its calf! I bet it'd taste like mashed potatoes!

Angels are made out of mashed potatoes. How long has *that* reality been out here?

Now, the other thing you have to think of is, are you going to go back into the same box you came out of? And, what if you go back into the wrong box, is that a problem?

OK, we're getting a little over our heads here. I'm going to back away from that.

So, well, let's review what we have: we have workers who won't share. So why don't we put them in a rickshaw together, put big English queenly hats on them, and have them share a bowl of mashed potatoes? That's something! That's a start! I don't think it's anything we should bust into the Oval Office with yelling, "Eureka!" just yet, but I think we see some common ground emerging here. You get people pulled around in carts wearing big crazy hats, knocking

back the smashers, and you've left a lot of hostility at the curb. I'm not saying it's *the* solution, but it's a solution we didn't have twenty minutes ago or however long we've been out here doing this. So, let's give it a shot! Let's get Defense and State on board! What have they got to lose?

So: thank you, Outside the Box! I'm sure we'll be back with many, many more challenging and complex problems for you to solve. Now I just have to find the box I came out of. ***(December 4, 2003)***

TWILIGHT CRUISE LINES.

[JAUNTY Sousa music swells, then plays under dueling VOICEOVERS.]
MAN: Mom and Dad aren't getting any younger, are they?
WOMAN: No they're not!
MAN: But what child wouldn't be thrilled to watch their parents sail off to exotic parts unknown?
WOMAN: To parts of the world they've only remotely heard about. And you'll never have to worry about them again, because we're Twilight Cruise Lines, with a whole new concept we call, "Senior Adventures in Maritime Careers."
MAN: But what will your relatives be doing? Well, a lot depends on their skills, attitude, and our demerit system. It could range from repeating the Captain's orders, to helping out around the boiler room.
WOMAN: And they'll be continually learning new skills, like cargo loading and unloading, cargo netting repair, and helping out around the boiler room.
MAN: How safe will your loved ones be with us? Well, we have a Costa Rican registry, and are subject to their laws, many of which even exceed the prisoner of war guidelines defined by the Geneva Convention! So you can cross that worry right off your list.
WOMAN: But what if you change your mind and want to get your parents back? Well, we'll be honest with you—it won't be easy. Say your parents met another couple while helping out in the boiler room, and they all became friends. How would you feel if the child of that other couple took these new friends away? It would leave your parents not only lonelier, but pulling double shifts of helping out around the boiler room.
MAN: So we make it pretty near impossible to even find us once we leave port. In fact unless you happen to own your own spy satellite, forget about ever seeing us again!
WOMAN: But let's accentuate the positive!
MAN: Get ready for some of the biggest vicarious thrills of your life, as you sit back and imagine the adventures your beloved elders will soon be living firsthand!
WOMAN: Bon voyage, Mom and Pop!
(October 24, 2003)

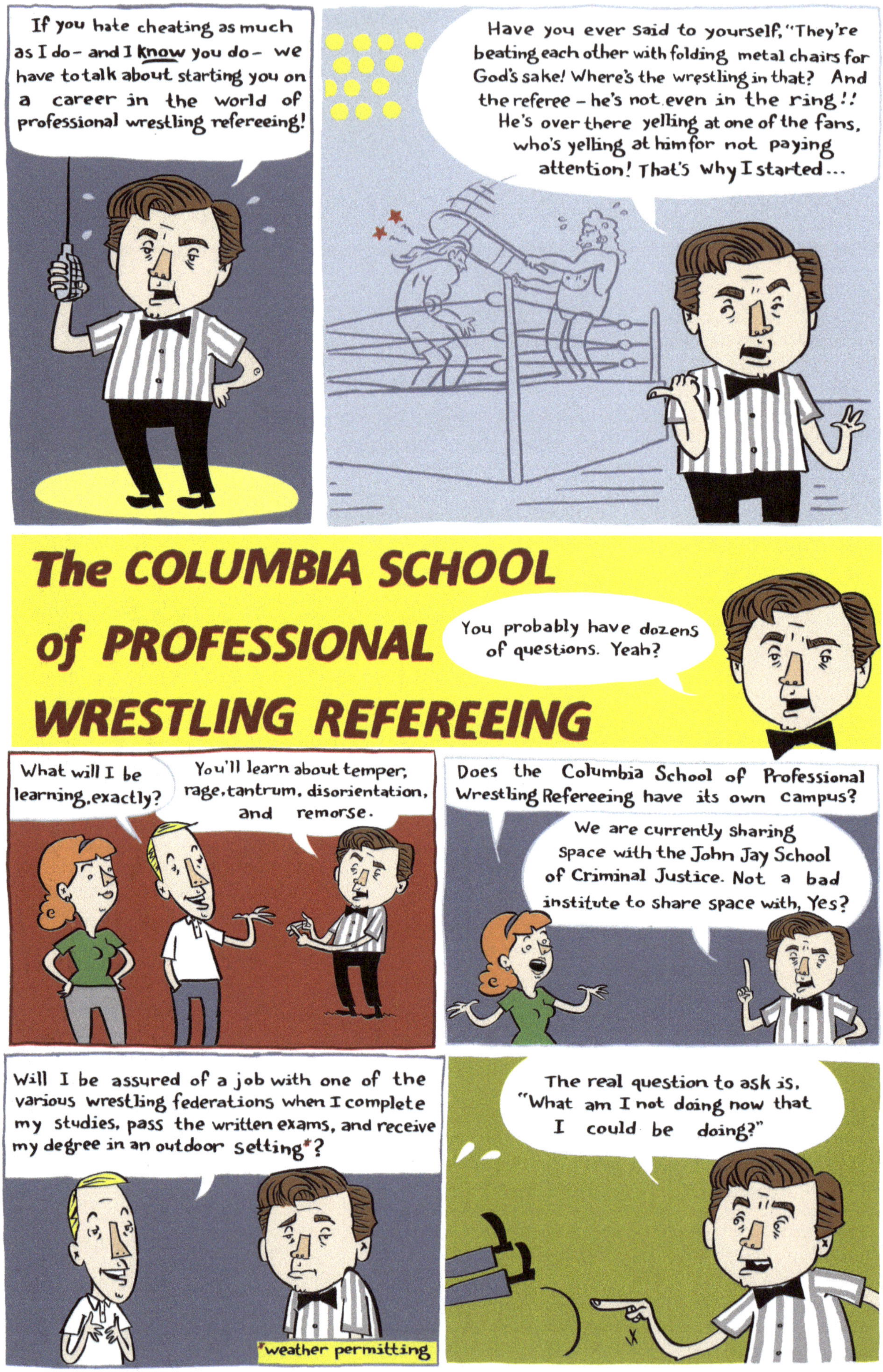
If you hate cheating as much as I do - and I know you do - we have to talk about starting you on a career in the world of professional wrestling refereeing!
Have you ever said to yourself, "They're beating each other with folding metal chairs for God's sake! Where's the wrestling in that? And the referee - he's not even in the ring!! He's over there yelling at one of the fans, who's yelling at him for not paying attention! That's why I started...
The COLUMBIA SCHOOL of PROFESSIONAL WRESTLING REFEREEING
You probably have dozens of questions. Yeah?
What will I be learning, exactly?
You'll learn about temper, rage, tantrum, disorientation, and remorse.
Does the Columbia School of Professional Wrestling Refereeing have its own campus?
We are currently sharing space with the John Jay School of Criminal Justice. Not a bad institute to share space with. Yes?
Will I be assured of a job with one of the various wrestling federations when I complete my studies, pass the written exams, and receive my degree in an outdoor setting*?
*weather permitting
The real question to ask is, "What am I not doing now that I could be doing?"

Originally broadcast on NPR March 21, 2002.
Illustration by **LANCE HANSEN**

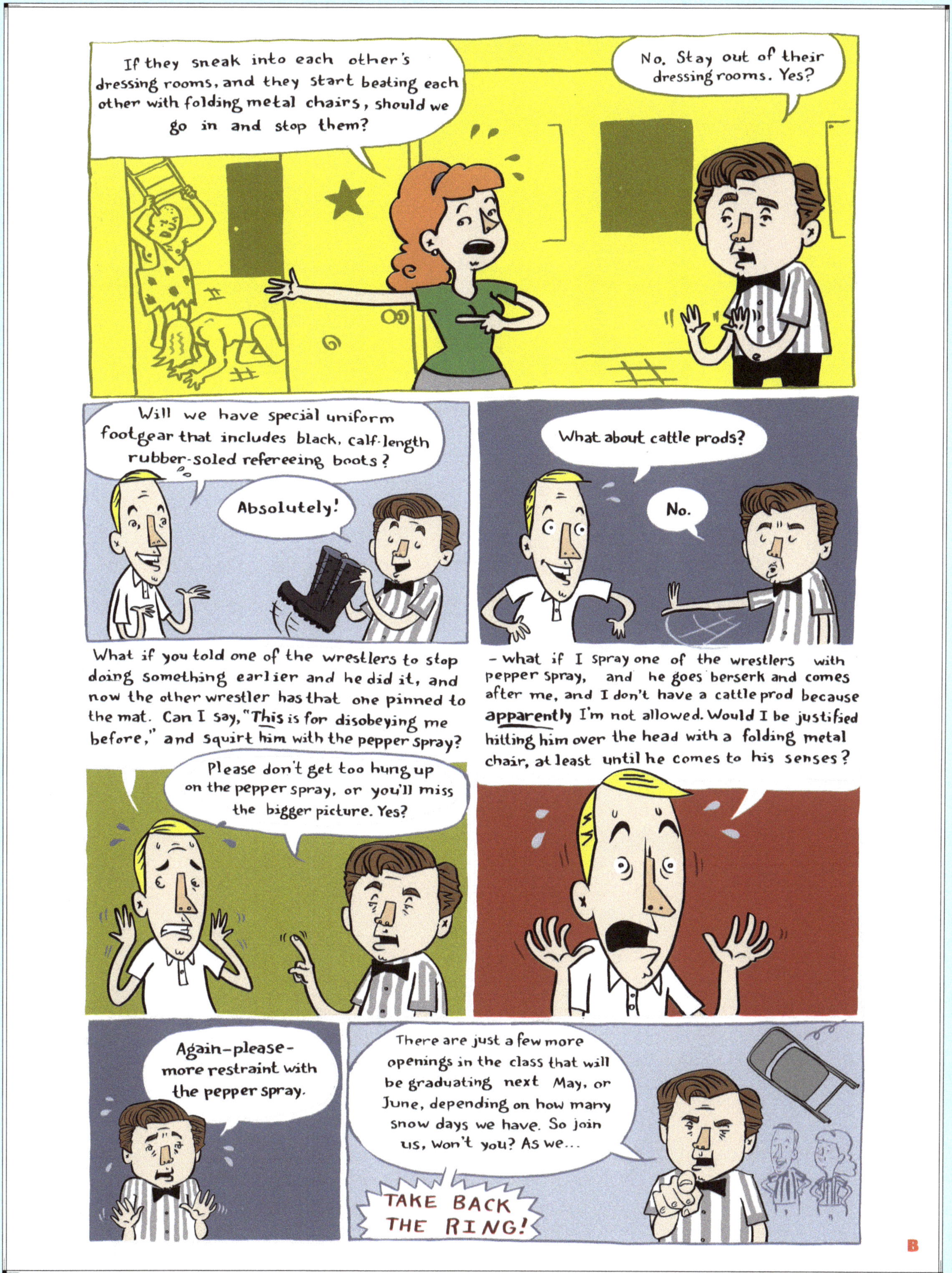
If they sneak into each other's dressing rooms, and they start beating each other with folding metal chairs, should we go in and stop them?
No. Stay out of their dressing rooms. Yes?
Will we have special uniform footgear that includes black, calf-length rubber-soled refereeing boots?
Absolutely!
What about cattle prods?
No.
What if you told one of the wrestlers to stop doing something earlier and he did it, and now the other wrestler has that one pinned to the mat. Can I say, "This is for disobeying me before," and squirt him with the pepper spray?
Please don't get too hung up on the pepper spray, or you'll miss the bigger picture. Yes?
- what if I spray one of the wrestlers with pepper spray, and he goes berserk and comes after me, and I don't have a cattle prod because apparently I'm not allowed. Would I be justified hitting him over the head with a folding metal chair, at least until he comes to his senses?
Again-please- more restraint with the pepper spray.
There are just a few more openings in the class that will be graduating next May, or June, depending on how many snow days we have. So join us, won't you? As we...
TAKE BACK THE RING!
B

"As a deeply uncomfortable depressed Midwest person, I relate to this excruciatingly hilarious book more than I'd like to admit."

—SAMANTHA IRBY,
New York Times best-selling author

"Hilarious, warm, relatable, confessional, and emotional. Her writing leaps off the page! But not literally. That would be horrible. Imagine writing leaping off the page, soiling your house. Just awful."

— MEGAN AMRAM,
writer/producer of
The Good Place & The Simpsons

ESSAYS on the AWKWARD, UNCOMFORTABLE, SURPRISINGLY REGULAR PARTS of BEING HUMAN

~ including ~

My Dog Explains My Weekly Schedule • Depression Isn't a Competition, but, Like, Why Aren't I Winning? • Mustache Lady • White Friend Confessional • Treating Objects Like Women

HarperOne   An Imprint of HarperCollins*Publishers*   www.harperone.com

PARLOR GAMES

BY BRIAN McCONNACHIE

WHO AM I?

C'mon, guess

I am friend to the working man and the part-time working man and the working woman on maternity leave with her feet up and the college girl on spring break at that place in Mexico they show on TV and makes her parents crazy with worry. I make the uniforms that people who have to wear uniforms wear. I write the songs that people bravely sing when they're looking through their closets wondering what uniform they're supposed to put on that day.

I steer the rigs. I drive the trains. I tug the boats. I fly the planes. I lower the gates at railroad crossings (but not when I'm driving the trains). So please, if you hear a train coming and you think I'm driving it and the gate is still up, for God's sake, stop! Use your heads, people. I can't be in two places at once. At least not under these figurative circumstances... well, actually, I can. But if I did it for your crossing, I'd have to do it for all the crossings and I just have too much on my plate right now. To say nothing about all the crap I have stored in my wheel house. Packed to the rafters. So let's just say I'd rather not and leave it at that.

Continuing on, I am both tomorrow and yesterday and I'm that Saturday that feels like a Sunday, because Friday was a holiday. I am a hot dog and a soda pop on a summer day; I am a mighty crown roast of veal with a pitcher of margaritas later that same evening. I am a car alarm, a smoke detector, a cell phone and a beeper all going off at once telling everyone in no uncertain terms: Switch to plan B! Hurry. I am the last cigarette lighter that still works on the Mir space station.

Do you still not know who I am? Really?

Okay, we can keep going. I have time.

How's this? I'm an enigma wrapped in an artichoke stuffed in a riddle dreaming of a powerful conundrum. Anything yet?

I am the determination that will finally compose the overdue official Song of Soccer that will be as jolly as "Take Me Out to the Ballgame" and will extoll the many wonderful bones of the foot while pooh-poohing the hand and all its fancy la-de-da digits in chorus after chorus after chorus. I am the midday calm following that summer day of hot dogs, crown roasts and margaritas when someone flings open the door and yells: Are you going to get up, or what?

I am the porter who takes your bags. I am the chambermaid who wonders: What the hell went on in here last night? I am sometimes with you and I am as often missing when you turn around wondering: was there someone standing behind me just now?

I am at the dry cleaners when you think I'm at the ATM and I'm at the DMZ having a BLT when you think I'm at the IRS. OMG! WHOA. Now, all of a sudden I'm turning into a mystery stapled to a riddle that's taped to a gypsy's thigh who stalks through the good farmer's artichoke patch wondering and wandering, wandering and wondering.

Do you know now? Still nothing? I'm running out of clues here.

What if I just said I was a dog sticking its head waaaaay out of the car window loving the breeze? You'd like that. I'd like that too but it's a little too dead on. Or is it?

Let's try this...

I am the frustration of a little child who can't get the top off the aspirin bottle and I am the happiness of another little child who has been inhaling nitrous oxide for the last four minutes. I am the ever-changing size of Greenland on world maps and every time you see me, you go quietly puzzled, thinking: Jeeze, look at Greenland! I don't remember it being that big. What do you suppose happened? I am the typos in your resume you were positive weren't there. I am the flammable string-in-a-can for people who are drunk at a wedding and think its amusing to shoot it at the bride and groom (though this is a part of me I am least proud of and rarely mention.)

Now, anybody? You've got that blank stare. I'll give you one last chance: I am the two-legged person hearing how the one-legged person's missing leg can still itch. Day after day the missing leg is itching and missing; missing and itching.

Still nothing? Okay. That's it. No more hints for you.

I am the "Handling," part of "Shipping and Handling," that you've always wondered about and has been robbing you blind for the last forty-eighteen years or so.

Surprised?

You shouldn't be.

RELIGION

BY BRIAN McCONNACHIE

THE DING-DONG HOODLUM PRIEST

God works in mysterious ways: an affinity for bra design, a devastating left hook

It's been years since I'd been in this church with Dan Mulroony and then it was to steal a statue of John the Baptist and dress him up as a crossing guard. But I'm back because he's now Father Dan Mulroony saying his first Mass. It's hard to imagine "Dukes" Mulroony, middleweight contender, as a man of the cloth. When that bell rang, he pounced like a cat and hit like a truck.

But boxing leaves deep scars.

Father Mulroony genuflected and descended the altar steps holding the Host in what were once punishing hands. I recognized some of the older folks now kneeling at the communion rail; their heads lifting back and their eyes blissfully closing as Danny gently placed the Eucharist on their tongues.

But just then, the great bell in the tower "BONG"-ed and suddenly Danny didn't seem to be in church anymore. He looked like he was back at Sunnyside Gardens. At the communion rail, Father Dan punched Mrs. Rodriguez in the mouth, sending her sprawling back a good twenty feet. Then Mr. Alvarez kneeling next to her caught a left cross that knocked two teeth from his head. Before Father Dan could connect with an uppercut to Mrs. Melch, two altar boys jumped on his back, and two other priests wrestled him to the floor. As they struggled, I ran up to help. Most of the congregation had fled to the rear of the church.

"Danny, look at me. Do you know me?" I said.

"Wh-where am I?"

"You're in Saint Bridget's, Danny." I pulled him to his feet.

"Why's everybody in the back of the church?" he said.

"They're afraid you'll slug 'em, Danny."

"Me? I just want to say Mass, give out communion, and hear confessions..." Then he yelled, "HEY! Come on back."

We grew up in the projects during tough times. The bra factory, where most everybody worked, had closed. No one had money. Our mothers would give us shopping lists and send us to Keppelman's to steal food. We'd load up with groceries and then break for the door. Keppleman hired bigger kids from other neighborhoods to stop us, but they didn't stop Danny. I once saw Danny—holding ten pounds of sirloin, two heads of romaine, some bell peppers, and a can of La Sueur peas—level four guys.

Then this cop, who was watching it all, came over. "Kid, you just knocked out 'Crazy Brains' McFee, the Golden Gloves champ! You ever thought of boxing?"

"Naw," Danny said, kicking a sirloin. "Boxing is for nincompoops. You get your brains scrambled. I want to be a bra salesman, or a bra designer. Basically, bra-related work."

"A lot of guys want that," the cop replied. "The field is crowded with guys. Smart guys. College boys and guys who'll work for nothing. The bra biz is a sucker's game, Danny."

About a month later, over in the railroad yards, Danny found a refrigerator car full of fresh avocados and artichokes. Somehow he got it off the tracks and pulled it all the way home when that very same cop stopped him.

"Hey, where do you think you're going with that railroad car, Danny?"

"Awww, lay off, will ya? I'm not bothering nobody."

"Son, I'll give you a choice: You can go to juvie jail or go into Golden Gloves."

"Can I design bras in juvie jail?"

"NO!" the cop yelled. "Nothing with bras there."

"Rats." Danny kicked an artichoke. "Okay...I'll box then."

It was the smart move. He was strong, had natural talent and went through opponents like a wrecking ball. At 19, he turned pro. But Danny hated to work. He was so gifted, he didn't think he had to.

"Danny, you got to train," his manager told him.

"Not now. I just got a great bra idea. Where's my pencil?"

His first few fights were against a bunch of palookas and he won easily. Then it got serious. "You're fighting Frantic Marvin next, then Filbert the Demented. Should you get by these seriously dangerous individuals, there is Insane Nigel, who they actually keep in an insane asylum. Danny," his manager warned, "you've got to be ready."

But Danny wouldn't listen, and took some bad beatings. After Danny's bloody whipping from Insane Nigel — who was taken away in a straitjacket — Father Doyle came to see him. He didn't have to say anything.

"I know, I'm through. What am I going to do?" Danny asked.

"Have you ever thought of becoming a priest?"

"Aww, that's for nincompoops and chumps."

"I'll be frank, Danny. You can become a priest and try to do some good in this world, or you can wind up in a sewer fighting alligators for scraps and probably get your hand chewed off."

"Which hand?" Danny quickly demanded.

"That one. The one you're always drawing bras with."

So Danny entered the priesthood. This time he worked hard and everyone was pulling for him. Our Danny, a priest!

Back in church, the congregation had slowly returned to the communion rail. I happened to glance at my watch and realized the noon bell was about to BONG.

"NO! DANNY WAIT!" This time it was all 85 pounds of Mrs. Torsalli who got flattened.

As I saw this, I thought I should probably hang around and warn that family scheduled for Father Dan's three o'clock baptism. They might want to get some headgear for the baby.

A BATTLE FOR ONE MAN'S SOUL!

MISSAL VS MUSCLE

FRI OCT 21

4 OTHER FIGHTS 4

FR. DAN MULROONY S.C.O.

"DUKES" MULROONY

FR DAN MULROONY
"MAN OF THE CLOTH"
vs
DUKES MULROONY
"THE HIBERIAN WINDMILL"

SUNNYSIDE GARDEN
Queens Boulevard & 45th St. L.I.C.

60¢ · $1.10 · $2.20 · $3.30 · 15 ROWS RINGSIDE $5.40 ALL INCLUDE TAX

BONNO '6

HELPFULNESS

BY BRIAN McCONNACHIE

A LETTER TO THE COMMISH

Never show the body of a drowned running back

Dear Roger:
What a delight meeting you at Denise's wedding.

I hope the new season has been a bit more fun for you than the last couple. I don't know if you were serious when you asked me if I had any ideas—maybe that was the open bar talking!—but if you're still in the market for brainstorms, I think I've got one.

If I correctly recall, you said the NFL's two biggest areas of concern are fatal concussions and female fans. Well, this little innovation should put every mother's worries to rest — but lose none of the excitement of abnormally strong men running at and from one another.

The players who have been murdering people in bars and elevators is a conversation for another day.

Here's the big picture: Instead of football cleats, the players will wear swim fins on their feet and they'll play the entire game in a foot and a half of water.

That's all there is to it. It's that simple and that's why no one has thought of it before. It's been right under our noses the whole time.

They'll galumph about throwing and catching and tackling each other while splashing away. Probably even some out-and-out laughing may ensue as the players pay witness to their own happy antics.

Then, when the defense least expects it — here's the bonus: Are you ready? — somebody does a "quick kick." Who wouldn't want to see someone in swim fins try and kick a football while standing in a foot and a half of water? The place will go berserk. The stadium announcer will have to tell the fans to please, in the name of God, calm down or the stadium will start to collapse.

What mother wouldn't want to see her son have some wholesome play in this version of professional football? What NFL coach could be more sincere when he tells his players, "...now get out there today and have some fun?"

But remember, it's still NFL football, except for the swim fins and the foot and a half of water. The fans will love it. The players and their mothers can, at last, start waving so-long to all that baffling brain damage.

But what if, you ask, a running back goes splashing up the middle, gets tackled and the whole defense piles on and won't get off and the runner is drowned?

What do you say to his mother?

Well first off, you're not going to say anything to anybody's mother because nothing like that will ever happen. NFL players wouldn't do that. Drowning the running backs is not in the culture.

But just in case, I've drawn up a contingency plan. I'm throwing this in for free, because I really want to see this happen.

How to Behave in the Unlikely Event of a Drowning: First, never show the body of a drowned player. You go right to commercial. Then quickly get the drowned player off the field by forming a sort of huddle around the body and then, with quick, little shuffle steps, head for the sidelines and start looking for a big box. Then, wait about two to three days, no sooner, so as not to alarm anyone. Then you visit the mother. Maybe bring two NFL vice presidents and a former player who brings along his Super Bowl ring and lets her wear it while they comfort her.

Continuing with this enormous unlikelihood, the mother now has to realize, accidents happen. Give her a lot of stats on how common drowning really is. The "hidden truth about drowning," sort of thing. The "silent killer from beneath the sea and beyond," that's nobody's fault.

So, getting back to the game, will the referees be wearing swim fins as well, you may ask?

No. They can wear their street shoes until the league decides what's the best thing to do here. Saddle shoes are always a stylish statement. Brogans might fill the bill. Just before the start of the second half, a ref should hold up one of his feet and show off his handsome wet shoe to the camera. An honest, human-interest moment. Plus, some women love anything to do with shoes.

I know that you know what all this says: It says some real life with normal people is going on here. How refreshing is that?

But back to the drowning. What about the so-called "criminal element"?

Again, there won't be any drownings! (Isn't that becoming clear by now?) Do you think for a moment the NFL is going to all the trouble of training athletes to run around in swim fins in a foot and a half of water, only to have a few bad apples jeopardize the whole operation?

Look who I'm asking. Will there be some pushback? Sure. But nothing we can't handle.

Roger, you more than anybody know you don't get to be the NFL in this life by neglecting the little things. There are still some matters, both big and small, to be decided. Do we use fresh water or salt? We tried using Gatorade, unfortunately it came off looking like urine. Beer's a natural, but that's a slippery slope to fall down; drunkenness and dare I say it, *accidental* drowning.

But this new football is coming, Roger. Coming to change the culture. Moms will be cheering. Players will be remembering where they parked their cars. Fans will be chanting, "More quick kicks!"

It's time to swim fin-up and make this magic happen.

Sincerely,
Brian McConnachie

P.S. Here are some new football markets and safer, less aggressive names you might also want to consider:
The Saratoga Springs Phillips Head Screw Drivers
The San Antonio Jumping Beans
The Hubba Hubba Tool and Dye Works
The Lakeview Paint Cans
The Florida Nap Time Boys
The Bricktown Clean Underpants Gang
...and I'm still working on some more. I'll keep in touch. — *B Mc.*

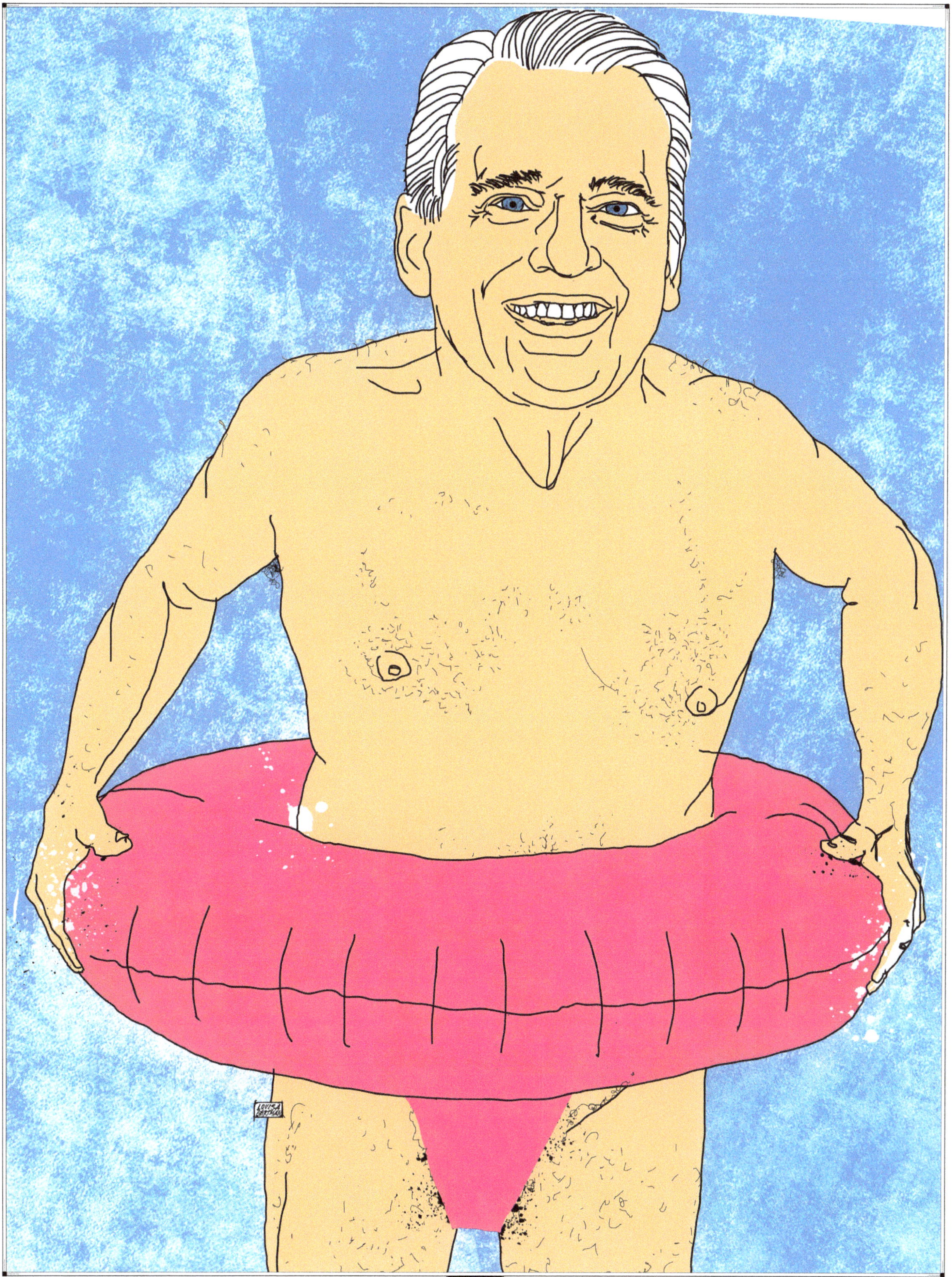
LOUISA BERTMAN

LOUISA BERTMAN

SELF-HELP!

BY BRIAN McCONNACHIE

INSPIRATIONAL ANIMAL STORIES #1: THE MOTIVATIONAL TIGER

Tiger, Tiger burning bright
Won't you guide my sleigh tonight?
—Edna St. Louis Missouri

If you don't stand up for yourself, no one else will. This was an important life lesson that a 600-pound Burmese tiger taught me one memorable afternoon at the Auto Show.

I had recently been fired from my job (after only two weeks) as a restroom attendant in a medieval adventure village. The reason they gave was that medieval villages didn't have restrooms much less restroom attendants and they weren't going to pay me. Before I could protest the logic of this, they had two guys in armor suits and swords escort me from the fairgrounds.

I felt small. It felt like I barely existed.

More and more, people were bumping into me and not saying, "Sorry." My dry cleaners started cutting all the buttons off my clothes and claiming I did it or my clothes didn't have buttons to begin with. The kids who'd throw water balloons at me and then run away didn't bother to run away anymore. They sauntered. And now all three of the waiters at the corner coffee shop spill soup on me. The manager agrees to pay for the cleaning but only if I use the same dry cleaners who cuts all my buttons off. And then my bank who said they "lost" my entire savings account—all the money my mother left me—and they weren't going to say a thing about it.

I really needed something to cheer me up and that's when I saw an ad for a car show. The latest in technology and style could be the thing I needed to take my mind off of my troubles.

As I looked at all the beautiful, futuristic cars, it really did take my mind off my woes. A number of the really expensive cars were on revolving platforms and some had gorgeous models posing with them. One of the cars, a $425,000.00 cream-colored Bentley convertible, had this awesome tiger sitting on the hood. I had never seen any creature so majestic and self-confident.

I moved closer and as I did, the tiger looked directly into my eyes. As strange as it sounds, I felt there was a sudden bonding between us. Then the platform's rotation moved the tiger from my sightline but then he came around and our eyes locked again. It was like I could read his thoughts. I could hear his thinking in my head. With each rotation he'd say something different like: I feel lonely. Am I an endangered species? Are you? Then it would go around again, our eyes would meet and he said: How is Siegfried's pal Roy doing? We all feel terrible about that. The next time around it was: Tell me that tigers aren't bad animals.

I was then getting a powerful feeling he was going to tell me something important. Something that could help me with my low self-esteem. I began to feel that the next time around he would say it. Or, I could even ask for his advice. But before I could, he said something I didn't expect: I'm getting dizzy. This sucks.

But when I saw him leap from the car, it became clear to me what he was saying. He was saying, Take action.

"Yes! I will!" I yelled at him. What happened next changed me in more ways than one.

As he landed on me, I went over backwards. There was no doubting what he meant by this: Life comes at you fast. "Boy! Doesn't it," I agreed.

His momentum rolled us over a few times. My initial understanding of this was: Turn over a new leaf. I felt I should probably be writing this down but that was a little impractical.

When his teeth went into my thigh, I felt oddly calm and went completely limp and from then on, everything seemed to move in slow motion. Then he shook me like a rag doll and tossed me up into the air. Now the toss in the air I got as: Reach for the heights. Go for the dream. Live your hope.

The violent shaking I wasn't too sure about. Shake things up? Wake up? Rip Life a new one? That was unclear to me and it hurt a lot.

Just before I went into a coma, I perceived another message from the tiger that was disturbing. Could this animal, instead of giving me helpful advice, for no good reason, be trying to kill me? Or perhaps he was telling me I should get a gun and kill my dry cleaner? Or the next person who bumps into me without saying, "Sorry"? When I woke up in the hospital all the positive lessons the tiger put into my head had a chance to settle down and form one clear plan. A plan of action and leaping and snatching that I'm going to execute as soon as I can get a pair of bouncy prosthetic legs.

The folks who ran the auto show said, as much as they would love to, they weren't allowed to give me any money for pain and suffering because they didn't have the right insurance.

But thinking back, I don't believe you can put a price on a motivational jolt that speaks to the good beast within us and turns our lives around. A chance like that comes once in a lifetime. If you're lucky. It's something I call "the tale of the tiger," and it's something you've just got to Geeerrrraaaab!— *Karl Raimes, age 31.*

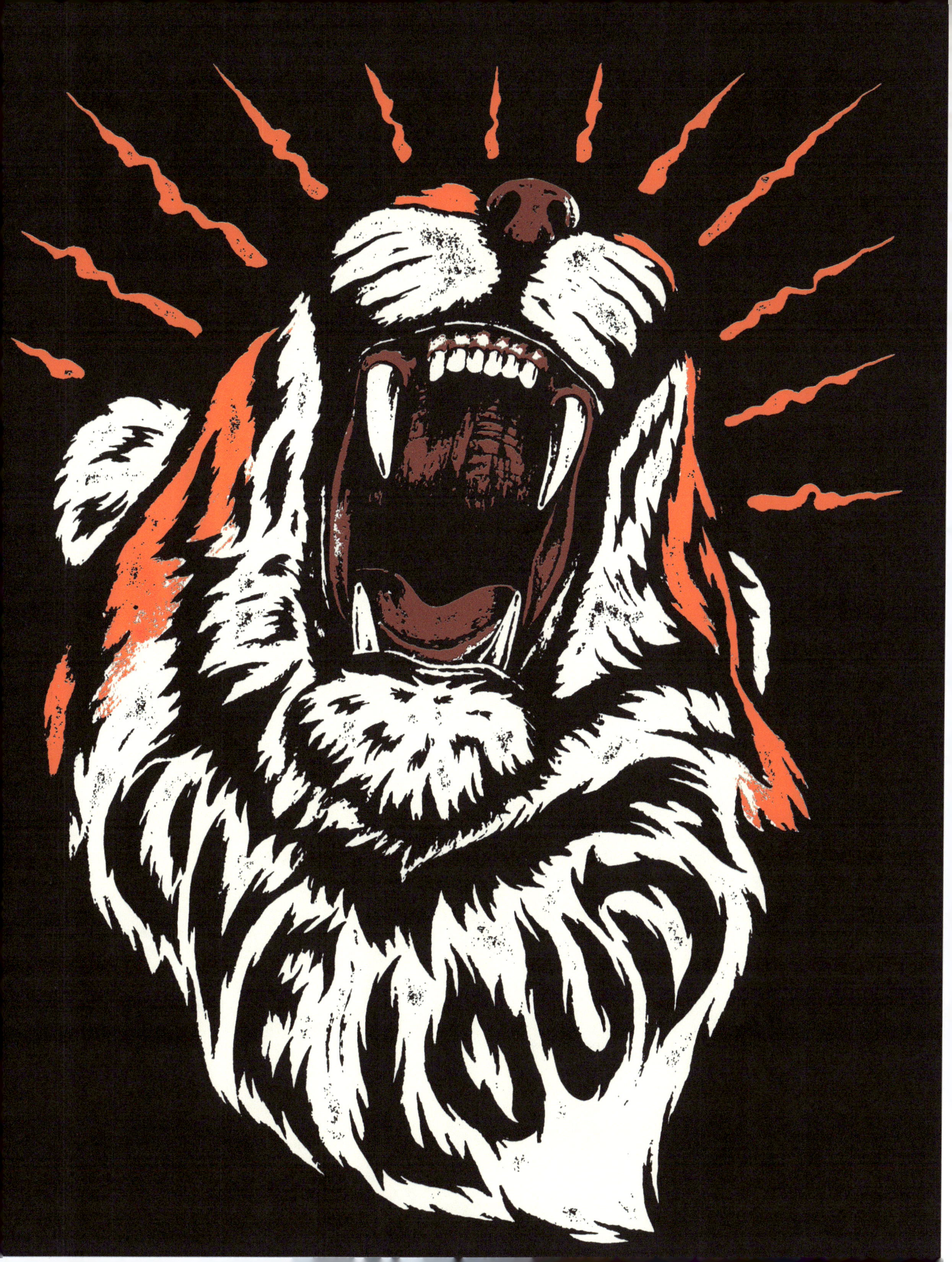

DOMESTIC ADVENTURES
BY BRIAN McCONNACHIE

CONNIE AND THE FIFTH TIME

I was not spying. I do not spy. Now or ever.

I'll never forget the first time I fell off the roof. *WhamThump! EEEOwww!*

It happened fast. One minute you're up on the roof, and the next thing you know, you're so not there at all anymore. *Whump!*

You don't get a lot of time to really examine the moments from when you've completely departed the roof but you haven't yet arrived upon the ground. It can really get away from you. Like, snap.

However, the second time I fell off of the roof, thump! Damn! It did seem to slow down more. I remember thinking, well, here I go; I'm falling off of the roof again. And I'm looking around for anything to grab onto. Then I happen to notice a lot of leaves in the gutters and make a mental note: don't forget to clean the gutters when you get back from the hospital. And for God's sake, try and be a little more careful up there.

By the third and fourth time I fell off the roof, it started slowing down quite a bit. I was hearing dogs bark and birds chirp and I could identify three different kinds of leaves: maple, elm and oak.

Now the sixth time I fell off the roof. *Thump Crapdamnpisshell.* I remember thinking, I should quit going up on the roof. But I did manage to savor the time immediately following the clawing desperately at the roof tiles but before the actual hitting the ground. I thought to myself, Hey, I'm in the air. It was that time I remember seeing four or five sparrows chasing a crow. The sparrows had good, quick looping moves and took turns pecking and all Mr. Crow could do was try and get the hell away. I wondered if any of them noticed me, still in the air, my arms flailing, and pondered, what's that thing doing? It was five sparrows I now recall. Then it was over pretty quickly. But while you're in the air, you learn to make that time last because, believe me, before you know it, *WHAM! Helldevilcrapfuck!* It's over.

Now the seventh, eighth and ninth times, I have to admit, sort of ran together. The tenth time really hurt when I landed. I guess we're talking about re-breaking the same bones again and again. But also the tenth time seemed to me by far the longest I spent in the air. There were lots of clouds that looked like they just came out of the dryer they were so white, clean and fluffy. I saw distinctive shapes. One of them had the body of a lion and the face of the Gerber Baby but then it turned into a sort of reclining buffalo. And then into a woozy version of Monument Valley. And then I think I saw the same crow but it was being chased by a whole different bunch of birds. Swallows?

Now if you're going to ask, what's with you going up on a steeply pitched Victorian farm house roof, sitting on the roof, walking around on the roof, traipsing around the roof and generally acting like the star from the show, *Fiddler on the Roof*, you're going to get a blank stare from me. And if there's one handy, I'll pick up a magazine and impatiently flip through it—rear to front—shaking my head that you don't get it and you're never going to get it and we don't have anything to talk about.

If you think I'm going to go into the "...there are two kinds of people in the world..." you're even more off-base.

However, if you were to ask me, by the way, what happened on the fifth time you fell off of the roof? Now that would get my attention. I would slowly close the magazine and put it down and regard you with a whole new level of respect.

Yes, that was no casual omission. That was the time Connie yelled at me.

When I fall off the roof, it's usually down the east side of the house onto the driveway near the juniper bushes and the grease trap. But on the fifth time, I went down the west side. And I fell past Connie's window. Connie is my wife; she has her own room. As I went by, I might have glanced in but it was too dark to really see anything and I certainly wasn't trying to see anything. I was falling off the roof for God's sake. Then I landed on the slate walkway near the irises. A few minutes later she came out of the house and stood over me for a while before she said anything.

"You were spying on me, weren't you? Don't ever do that again, hon. It'll really make me crazy and you don't want me crazy." Then she headed out the driveway, got into somebody's waiting van and took off. I couldn't see who was driving.

Spying on her!

As best I could, I yelled after her that spying is not exactly something you achieve by trying to see in someone's window you're falling past at that incredible speed that falling things all travel at. I'm certain anyone who has ever had any success at spying can verify that fact. Spying is a real dig-your-heels-in kind of chore. It's not done on the fly. If I had been able at that moment to drag myself into the house, I would have gotten the Policy Director of the CIA on the phone to verify that their spies do not jump off roofs or out a window to grab a peek into another window. Even for a government that's not exactly known for being cost-conscious, that would be a pretty inefficient use of their highly trained personnel.

I was not spying. I do not spy. Now or ever. But that was the fifth time.

I had to make a compromise with Dr. Goldberg or he swore he wouldn't be my doctor anymore. I had to promise I'd only go up on the roof if there was an absolute roof emergency. Or if there was a flood and the whole house was floating away. Connie and I could sit on one of the dormers tightly holding onto one another. A little scary but romantic.

We didn't go too deeply into what would constitute a "roof emergency," but as soon as they take these screws out of my jaw and forehead and the brace comes off of my head, I'll be able to sit at the kitchen table and make up a list of what would "constitute" a "roof emergency." A loose weather vane would probably qualify. That'd be one.

...that is, if we had a weather vane up there...

AMERICAN ORIGINALS
BY BRIAN MCCONNACHIE

JOHNNY BULLWHIP
If he wore a number, they would've retired it.

Johnny Bullwhip. He was the fastest bullwhipper in the territory. He was fast and accurate and amazing. No one could beat Johnny Bullwhip in a bullwhip fight. No one handled a bullwhip like him. And if you weren't too particular about spelling, he could bullwhip your name right into your face. Unless you had a name like Alexander or Jedidiah, which might not fit. But he could make an "Al" or a "Jed" if you really had your heart set on it.

Long ago people stopped challenging him to bullwhip fights. No one stood a chance. Johnny Bullwhip could bullwhip the down out of a baby's ear without waking the little darling. And did, too (with the mother's permission).

He wore a bullwhip on each hip, another bullwhip, like a belt, at the small of his back and a little, teeny bullwhip—actually, it was more like shoelaces—on the side of his boots.

If Johnny Bullwhip had worn a number, they would have retired it.

But these days he spends most of his time lecturing about bullwhips and taking care of your bullwhip, bullwhip registration, bullwhip safety goggles, proper cleaning, oiling and winter storage of your bullwhips.

Still, there's always some kid, some punk, who comes along and has to challenge Johnny Bullwhip to a bullwhip fight. Johnny usually says, "Put your bullwhip away, son. I don't do that anymore." But do you think they listen? Of course not. They have to learn the hard way. In a bullwhip fight. Against the fastest, sharpest, nicest, toughest bullwhip cracking guy in all of bullwhipdom. And small leather beltdom as well—if it ever comes to that.

But it never does.

I caught up with Johnny last month, at the Woodward County (OK) Regional Bullwhip and Pontoon Boat Show. Johnny's getting on in years, as we all are, and there are those who would say he's losing his touch. "His touch," no. His bullwhips, sometimes. He'll forget where he puts them.

…But if you're thinking of challenging him, I wouldn't count on it. —BM

Have you ever whipped a bull that didn't deserve it? That's a good question. You know, you start out whipping bulls and then you get to a point where you have to ask yourself, do any of them really deserve it? You don't know. You get the call from your agent and he gives you an address of a farmhouse somewhere in west Texas and you just show up and start in. "Tell it to the whip." That's a question everyone who's ever cracked a bullwhip has to answer for him or her self.

What's the main difference between bull riding and bull whipping? Another good question…In one you actually get on the bull and try to ride him around. Try to get him to go where you want him to go. Maybe even get the bull to do a little high-step prancing like show horses do. With the other, you just beat him, bam, bam, bam.

Do you, Johnny Bullwhip, make your own clothes or do you find someone who can make them for you and threaten to beat them, whip them thoroughly, if they don't make you a nice suit of clothes? I've tried that. Yes. I think all bull whippers have tried that at one time or another. It doesn't work. And it's wrong. You beat someone with a bullwhip and they're not going to sit down and sew you a nice suit of clothes. They're shaking. Their judgment is off. No, it doesn't work. It's wrong on a lot of levels.

Is it always wrong to bring anger to a bull whipping? I think so. Yes. Some people say, "use that anger." But I think it's something you leave outside the barn door. Or what's that place outside the barn.

The…barnyard? No. Like that. The, ah…thing with the wood…and the gate.

The corral? Yes!…in the corral. Leave the anger in the corral and just pay attention to the whipping. Some people have to keep reminding themselves: It's business. It's not personal. It's not about you, it's about the bull and the whip. And the lessons you can only hope the bull is learning from the whipping you're giving him.

Johnny Mango once said, in a rare encounter, that he… Please. Johnny Mango!

He said that he hit you really hard on the back of the neck with a mango, and you were all disoriented and then blacked out before you could get to your bullwhips. Not a word of that is true. He missed me—completely. And it was a papaya. How more wrong can one sentence get?

Well, his name is Johnny Mango. He's noted for throwing mangos from secret hiding places. No. His name is Something Something Cabrini. Do you know how he operates? He either hides in the bushes, up in a tree or in a ditch by the road and when you're facing the other direction, he throws a papaya at the back of your neck. And then resumes hiding. He does throw hard but his aim isn't any good. As to why he does this, hey, your guess is as good as mine. I see nothing heroic in this.

If you ask him, he'll roll out some line of crap about fighting crime. What he needs is a normal job and someone to teach him the difference between a mango, a papaya and a guava. Different members of the *plantae* family. Ask him about that.

That brings me to the question: in the family of Johnnys, you and Johnny Guitar are generally regarded as the most senior and respected members. What do you think of this new guy, Johnny Mimosa? Yeah. I think I've heard of him. What does he do exactly?

He orders a double mimosa, then throws it in somebody's face and gets into a fight over it. He wins about half the time. That sounds promising. There's a place to plant your flag. I think we're done here. No more questions. I'm not going to comment on Johnnys gone rogue.

Thanks for your time, Mr. Bullwhip.

THE DAIRY RESTAURANT

BEN KATCHOR

"KATCHOR SEES INTO THE LIFE OF EVERYTHING HE TOUCHES.... Nothing fails to interest him. I want to sit next to nobody but him on my next international flight."
—ALEXANDER THEROUX, AUTHOR OF *DARCONVILLE'S CAT*

Through text and drawings, award-winning author Ben Katchor retells the history of where we choose to eat and illuminates the historical confluence of events and ideas that led to the proliferation of dairy restaurants in America.

"This GRAPHIC HISTORY shows again Katchor's gimlet eye for CURIOUS CONNECTIONS and obsessive attention to detail."
—PUBLISHERS WEEKLY

"An informative, NOSTALGIC evocation of a SPECIAL urban dining experience."
—KIRKUS REVIEWS

A UNIQUE HISTORY of a beloved culinary institution

Schocken
>nextbook

Potty training can be a PRICKLY issue.

Laugh out loud with this picture book about a family *attempting* to potty train their new pet porcupine, from *New Yorker* cartoonist Tom Toro. You may almost wet your pants giggling.

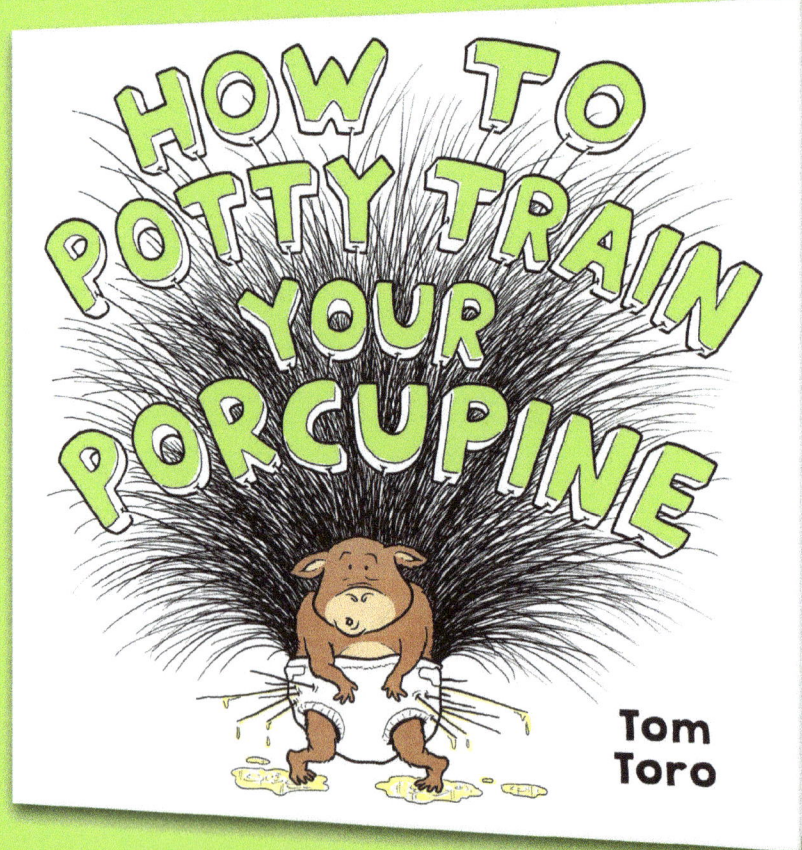

 LITTLE, BROWN AND COMPANY
BOOKS FOR YOUNG READERS #HowtoPottyTrainYourPorcupine | LBYR.com

BRIAN McCONNACHIE

Wigglesworth

"Quit staring out the window and tend to your labors or I'll box your damn ears, you great, worthless oaf!"

What we did to Wigglesworth was mean. But what he's been doing back has been psychotic.
I'll take some blame for starting it.
Bill and I.

Bill Sodarman was my cubie here at Value-Content Plus—an odd name for a niche greeting card company, wouldn't you agree?

The trouble started with Bill being a huge fan of the film *Lawrence of Arabia*. We both were—but Bill could quote the whole movie. He wanted to be Lawrence of Arabia. Whenever he'd head out he'd usually pause in the doorway, punch his fist in the air and demand, "For whom do we ride?"

Then I'd yell, "We ride for Lawrence!" (pronounced "El-Orence.") Sometimes, if spirits were high, other cubies would chime in and we'd all yell, "On to Aqaba!" Then off he'd go, which was usually home for dinner.

That was his bit; my bit was to announce, as I angrily dialed the next client on my call sheet: "These people want their freedom and I'm going to give it to them!"

But in time, it grew stale. We needed something new. Then one day we heard about a new guy, an illustrator, who recently came to work over in the Art Department. His name was Osgood Wigglesworth.

I don't know why, but I couldn't say it enough. "Osgood Wigglesworth"—it reminded me of some old-timey radio show. Wigglesworth was the underdog who always got screwed over for one specious reason after another, while his boss unloaded savagely on him.

"Have a care, Wigglesworth...Don't think we're not onto you, Wigglesworth...Blast you Wigglesworth, where are those top secret reports? Did you take them to the place of your birth, Wigglesworthtonville?"

Soon, T.E. Lawrence was a memory; now, Bill and I took turns chewing each other out. "Wigglesworth, quit staring out that window and tend to your labors or I'll box your damn ears, you great, worthless oaf."

It was great fun.

Bill and I are in sales. The guts of the joint, we like to think. The Golden Guns, the Death from Above Boys, snug in our F-22 Raptors. We'd bag the prey; they'd skin and clean it. We had rank and influence. People looked up to us. We had a lifetime seat at the cool kids' table. (As if Value-Content Plus had a cool kids' table.)

As I said, we're a niche outfit. Some of our better sellers have been: "Water Awareness Day"; "Great-Great-Grandmother's Day"; "Christmas Is Coming"; "Happy Good Friday"; "Genital Awareness Week"; "We Heard You Put Down Your Ferret, Sorry"; "Your Baby is Certainly Interesting-Looking Day"; "Men Who Get Women's Diseases Awareness Month"; "We Heard Your Bike Was Stolen, That Sucks"; "Your Cat's Not Looking Well"; "We Hope They Find a Cure for Whatever It Is You Have." Crap like that. We leave the heavy emotional lifting to Hallmark.

Our supervisor was a shy and uncomfortable man, totally unlike the boss we created for our Wigglesworth saga. Our real boss rarely came around, but when he did, he'd limit his conversation to "How's it going, men?" and "Keep up the good work, fellas." Usually we'd ignore him, or give him a grunt with a forced smile, like: *Do you mind? We're trying to get work done here.*

On one of these visits Bill had skipped his a.m. meds and was looking pretty manic, and reverted to some standard *L. of A.* scripture. Our boss never understood any of it—but then, what's to understand? It's just guys at work screwing around and making crap up because we're good at it and the days can get pretty goddamn long around here if you haven't figured that out yet. Though we don't usually make our supervisor the butt of anything, once in a while we'll include him; he seems to love that. On his last visit, he even seemed to be waiting for it, wanting to be included in our merry band.

After an uncomfortable silence, our supervisor asked, "Is there anything...you guys...want to say...to me?" Then, like a football coach expecting the Gatorade bath, he braced himself, eyes squeezed shut.

Bill slowly rose; the beast had awakened. "I carry twenty-three great wounds all gotten in battle," he said in a tone of deep, icy anger. "Seventy-five men I have killed with my own hands in battle. I burn my enemy's tents. I take their herds. The Turks pay me a golden treasure. Yet I am poor, because" (long pause) "I...AM A RIVER TO MY PEOPLE."

Bill pulled a drawer from a desk and flung it, almost taking off an intern's head. Then I jumped up on my desk and ululated, inflating it with all the joyful madness I could. A bunch more cubie voices joined the howling. Then came the synchronized desk-pounding and foot-stomping.

"Whoa!" our supervisor said. "Everybody calm down. No reason for this! Shhhhhh. Come on now." Then, with the cries still echoing, he headed off as aimlessly as he arrived. Reminding himself to skip that approach in the future.

The Sales Department worked out of a huge warehouse. How huge? It could probably accommodate a dozen C-5 cargo transports and have room left over for a Costco, a Walmart and the Goodyear blimp. The company picked up this property for next to nothing and even gets State and Fed tax credits for using it, and additional money for hiring people it doesn't need to keep it clean. We have a huge janitorial staff.

Judging from our surroundings, the place was probably an airbase where they tested nuclear weapons. There isn't a sprig of vegetation within twenty miles of the buildings. We're just out here in the desert, by ourselves, creating screwy greeting cards for bogus occasions that people with sad lives and no friends should buy, but too often manage not to.

So, I get a call to report to Accounting to once again explain the mysterious twists and larky turns of my expense account. Accounting also uses up just a portion of another super-sized building away on the other side of "The Campus." I have to drive there; it's like, five miles away.

Our entire operation could fit in a corner of one of these garguantuan fever dream hangars. But some nincompoop decided, back in the day, "Hey, we have the room, let's use every goddamn foot of it!"

For shorter trips around The Campus, we have some old golf carts available—or would, if someone (Hey Bill, are you reading this?) would remember to recharge the batteries every now and then. These carts are only supposed to be for senior management (who we decided includes Bill and I) and those Board of Directors members who regularly take the trip out here because they still don't trust the mail or bank wire transfers so they come here personally to pick up their quarterly checks. Most board members are retired military officers or former Congressman in their eighties who double as lobbyists and are relatively worthless at getting our special brand of dim-witted, holiday happiness onto the Federal calendar.

So, as I'm heading out to Accounting, I realized: Accounting is not that far, maybe three miles, from the Art Department. Home of our new, secret best friend, Osgood Wigglesworth.

I wasn't sure what exactly I'd say to him. What if things got ugly? Wigglesworth might be a former cage match fighter who detested interruptions as much as he hated being called "Wigglesworth."

At last, I found his cubie. (The Art Department is the size of a football field.)

He was bent over his drafting table, lost to his surroundings. I opened big. *"Wigglesworth!"* I shouted. *"Blast your worthless hide!"*

He jumped a foot in the air and I saw in an instant he was perfect. Fundamentally nervous, overly dressed and fearful of authority, he had a high forehead and

prominent ears. You simply couldn't wish for a better Wigglesworth. There was both shyness and sadness to him. He was obsequious. And the topper: he wore a little red PeeWee Herman tie.

"Where are those sketches of Desi Arnaz for National Hispanic Achievement Day?" I said. "Dammit, Wigglesworth, if you put that market in harm's way, we'll feed you to the hounds and then the wolves, Wigglesworth."

He nodded emphatically and kept muttering, "Yes! Desi Arnaz. Immediately." By the careful way he repeated the name, it seemed apparent Wigglesworth had never seen *I Love Lucy*. "Yes, sir, I'll get right on it...Desi Arnaz. I'll work from photographs..."

"Well, don't just stand there arguing with me..." I hurried away before he could ask me anything that might be of help in this, his time of emergency.

When I got back to Sales, I informed Bill that Wigglesworth was now working for us. "What'll we do with him?"

"We'll think of something," said Bill.

The next morning Bill zeroed in on The Old Wigglie-diggle. He paused at the entrance and did a long slow burn, not unlike Desi gives to Lucy when the trouble she's started has come home to roost.

Then, with a growl, Bill cleared his throat and erupted.

"Blast you Wigglesworth! Have you learned nothing of our popular and modern ways?" Bill shouted.

Wigglesworth probably detected the same urgency in Bill's voice as in mine. He appeared to know it was coming from the same place and was prepared.

"Here you go, sir," he said, handing Bill prototypes with beautifully rendered drawings. In one, Desi was helping Fred Mertz fix a plumbing problem; then Desi, wearing an apron and flipping a hamburger; then Desi helping a blindfolded child strike a piñata; then Desi carefully eating a taco, so as not to get any on his new white shirt. Wigglesworth must have been up all night diligently watching reruns, taking notes, and drawing.

This shut Bill up, but not for long. He gave a quick look, then was struck by an inspired reply.

"Why you sneaky bastard! This isn't Desi Arnaz. This is *Ricky Ricardo*. What are you pulling, Wigglesworth, a fast one? Well, you'll not get a fast one past me, you filthy bastard!" said Bill.

"I'm through coddling you. We all are, Wigglesworth—if that really is your name, and it's not Peabody or Ignatz Dinglehoover—because we're on to *that* ruse as well. You fix this mess or I'll turn you over to Division, by God, and let them have at you! Believe me, you won't like that one bit. What Division has up their foul sleeve when it comes to dealing with a Sneaky Pete like you, why it makes me shutter and twitch." Bill shuddered and twitched a bit, then left.

Now, what we didn't know was happening was, in a building many, many miles away the hazing we'd started had been taken up by people who overheard us. It began in the Art Department. Then it spread to Accounting. Even people from the janitorial staff showed up to take some cheap shots at Mr. W.

When I heard of it, my first criticism was on style: they had none. They'd say things like, "Hey, Wigglesworth, you're a tool," and "Hey, stinky, you stink," and "Hi, you stupid moron." That's all they had. Absolutely no thought went into it. It was lazy and rude.

The closest thing to a premise was: blame him for every conceivable wrong that happened to the company. If there was inclement weather that kept people away from card stores, it was Wigglesworth's fault. If Hallmark's latest TV show got a decent *TV Guide* review, it was Wigglesworth's fault.

This continued for a while.

Then one day, out for a drive, I was stopped at our one and only four-way stop. There were two cars: me, heading north, and one heading east, surrounded by vast desert. Then I noticed the other driver was Wigglesworth. I waved. He looked awful.

"Hey O.W.! How's it going, man? Where are you heading? I've never been up that road."

"Oh, it's you," he said. "Tell your pals, especially that Sputnik Monroe character, it's over. I'm heading to Division myself. I'm not afraid anymore. Things are going to change around here."

"'Division!' Okay," I said, cheering Wigglesworth on. "Yo Division! That's where the big magic happens. I hear ya, O.W. Give 'em hell!"

He shot me an odious little look, and before I could assure him, "Hey man, I'm on your side," he sped off.

Now there is no, "Division," of course. Bill made that up. But I read it as Wigglesworth trying to fight back, in the spirit of things. Good for him. It just might put the kibosh on all the witless needling.

And it did!

Some time later, the CEO of Value-Content Plus, Thaddeus J. Ethalrod, who lived in a gated Florida community and only communicated by e-mail, announced that Osgood Wigglesworth has just been made the head of R & D and would be relocating to Division. He would, from today, report directly to the Chairman.

"Wigglesworth," the CEO wrote, "is a hard-working, multi-talented, brilliant fellow and has some exciting ideas we'll be soon implementing." Then, at the bottom of the e-mail, in a larger typeface: "Sputnik Monroe is ordered to report to Division immediately."

"I don't mean to be rude, but are you Sputnik Monroe?" I asked Bill.

"I was going to ask you the same thing. What do you think Sputnik did?"

That afternoon, I took a spin around the Art Department, to see if I could find out some scuttlebutt. Nobody knew anything. Sputnik Monroe, whoever he was, didn't work in the Art Department.

And neither did Wigglesworth. His cubie was cleared out. The only trace of his ever being there were his finely crafted illustrations of Desi Arnaz (or Ricky Ricardo, I forget which) ripped to shreds and still in his wastebasket.

One morning Bill asked me, "Do you think it would be a good time for me to put in for a raise?" He'd already taken it up with our boss, and our boss, without even looking up, told him to "take it up with Division. They seem to be running everything these days."

I told Bill he should wait until the vernal equinox lines up with the harmonic convergence, hoping to squeeze a laugh out of him.

"I'm serious," he said. He bombarded me with reasons why Division wouldn't, couldn't refuse him this raise. His numbers were excellent. Our pal, our very own creation, Sir Wiggle-Dee-Doo was being groomed for greatness. Now was the perfect time. But Bill couldn't make himself do it. "I'm terrified," he said.

"You do realize you made up Division? Give yourself a raise."

"Maybe I did and maybe I didn't," Bill said. "But I'll tell you: you don't want to be on the wrong side of history when push comes to shove and Division is the only thing standing between you and the barbarians!" he said.

"Is that from a movie?"

I always saw Bill as a wiser, older brother. I wanted us to be together on this, whatever "this," was. But he was clearly rattled, and that rattled me, too.

Then later, another e-mail from Chairman Ethalrod The Annoying. It announced Wigglesworth has been on special assignment and has reported back: if we ever hope to overtake Hallmark, we might need to enlist the help of the American Greeting Card Company. They're an angry people and maybe we can channel some of that "anger" to our benefit.

Hold it. "Overtake Hallmark"?

What demented brain did this escape from? We have a successful philosophy regarding Hallmark. It goes like this: *Keep the Fuck Out of Hallmark's Way Or They'll Beat the Shit Out of You*. We're not particularly proud of the inelegant wording, but it's served us well and kept us in business through good times and bad and now is not the hour to abandon its golden truth. There are plenty of culverts, air shafts and alleyways throughout this great land littered with the teeth, fingers and toes of those who once dared dream the dream they'd like to "Overtake Hallmark."

As to AGC, we know they are not a pleasant people. There were about sixty of them who showed up and each smelled worse than the one before. They wore ill-fitting uniforms that made them look like they recently escaped from an eighth-grade production of *The Yeomen of the Guard*.

Practically overnight Value Content Plus and the Ameican Greeting Card Company struck an alliance. If one was attacked by Hallmark, both would respond in kind. Mostly with baseball bats, pitchforks and rocks for the first assault, then running each other over with cars for the second. I guess? It was not made clear what the boundaries were, which is of concern because AGC is absolutely evil and crazy. We should really join up with Hallmark and elimanate AGC.

But Division felt otherwise. We would be under the command of AGC, which took little time establishing their authority over us. They sent two platoons and a support group. We were all re-assigned to five-member teams.

It didn't matter what your job was before. Each team had to come up with a new holiday; the background of that holiday; create meals to be eaten on that holiday; and make colorful costumes to be worn—with extra holiday uniforms for our senior overseers to wear.

Interestingly, there was no mention of greeting cards. But the message was crystal clear: we were all going to have to sew uniforms—by hand—for these smelly monsters.

The goons from AGC ordered all the walls of our cubbies to come down—there would be no more privacy. "Privacy breeds dirty deeds," they kept reminding us. Also we were not to make any eye contact with our overseers. Such would be a punishable offence. And the classic: only speak when spoken to.

A lot of them carried riding crops, which was pointless. Physical violence will never be an incentive for people at a niche greeting card company, who are frankly having a tough enough time in life as it is.

Then one morning, the whole company got an email: "Hallmark has gotten word of our alliance," it read, "and they are not happy about it. They claim it's a provocative act." That was alarming, but worse was yet to come. The email was signed "O.S. Wigglesworth, Deputy C.E.O.

One day, a new notice went up, SPUTNIK MONROE DAYS MISSING: 53. BRING US THE FORESKIN OF SPUTNIK MONROE.

I kicked my roll-y chair back from my desk and said to Bill, "Should Mr. Monroe still be in possession of said foreskin, that would seem a bit harsh, wouldn't you agree?"

Bill didn't laugh; he never laughed anymore. He looked gray. "I bet Monroe is long gone by now."

"Gone as in 'escaped,' or gone as in…"

"However you want to take it," Bill said.

A week later a rumor circulated: one of our elderly board members, a retired Army Colonel, age eighty-three, made a fuss about being paid late. This complaining, the rumor said, earned him two punches in the stomach and one kick in the pants. Was it true?

It was certainly true that they confiscated all of Cathy Myers's dolls. She's from Accounting and is a total sweetheart. We've all been telling her; let it go and calm down. This will all be over one day.

I found myself thinking, "If I can just speak to Wigglesworth, I think I can walk a lot of this back." Quietly, person-by-person, we put together a small delegation to sneak out of the barracks at night and have a talk with Wigglesworth. But it didn't happen; no one knew where Division was.

I learned a lot. Like, for example: It's really unnerving if you're trying to thread a needle with one eye shut and the tip of your tongue protruding and …WHAM! Down comes the whip on the table. "Faster!" the goon says, and you try to ignore all the mistakes and go faster. What else are you going to do?

I think that's the kind of thing that made Bill take off. He didn't say anything to me, just one day he wasn't there. To pass the time, I developed a crush on Cathy. I know it can never be. This is just the kind of thing AGC was trying to stop when it removed all the cubies.

What a lousy time to fall in love! But the heart will have its way.

So that's where we are today. Bill is still missing. Word is he's hiding in a sewer tunnel under one of the barracks. In a way, I'm glad. I'd hate to see him, a man who once symbolically rode with Lawrence to Aqaba—a man who was a river to his people!—be forced to sew clown clothes for bad people. Yes, my brother. Run.

It turns out, I like making capes. I'll tell you something that's pretty universal: Everyone loves wearing a cape. People can deny it all they want. They can jump up and down and swear it's not true, but that won't change anything. You give a man a cape and a gun, and within minutes, he'll be wearing the cape, swooping around, totally ignoring the gun.

Word has it Hallmark has been chartering busses left and right, and they are on their way. They should arrive by tomorrow, around noon.

To prepare, AGC has got us out in the desert, collecting rocks. They are blazing hot. I pick one up, put it in the bag as fast as I can. My thumbs are beginning to blister.

Guess who just rode by? Ol' Wigglesworth! He's on horseback, encouraging us. I had my thumb in my mouth, so I was slow on the salute. Wigglesworth gave me a smart one across the shoulders.

"Sorry," I said. "Picking up these rocks really hurts."

"Certainly it hurts," Wigglesworth said. "The trick is not *minding* that it hurts."

The Masked Wrestlers of Mexico
by Seymour Chwast

A set of six, signed, 8.5" x 11" giclée prints on archival paper. Inspired by the revered tradition of Mexican wrestlers wearing creative and menacing masks.

Limited edition prints. Each set of six, $350.

Purchase Online at
www.pushpininc.com/gallery/pushpin-products

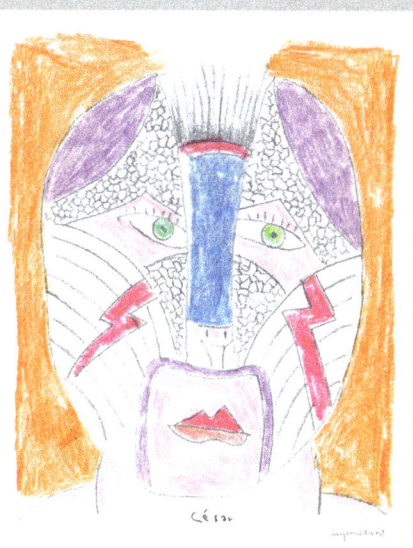

McCONNACHIE to BROWN

Brian McConnachie and I have been friends since the early '70s, when I began selling cartoons to **The National Lampoon**. *After Mike asked me to contribute to this issue, I went back through all the letters Brian had written to me over the years; they were so charming and funny that I wanted to present some excerpts. I hope you enjoy them as much as I did.*

MK Brown

Movie revenues would have to quadruple to equal the money made from the car theft industry. Just a thought.

— I've taken up painting. I'm starting with horse's hooves. And I'm going to stay with horse's hooves.

I'm finishing a one act Play you'd like. It involves people who live under Grand Central Station and worships Miss Subway — Some of it isn't pretty

One June in the Year of the Utah Mud Runs

totally missed ice skating this winter. I'll shoot for fishing this Summer.

I have finished the script and will turn it in during the first week of May. I'm pleased with it. It has everything in it but monkeys. It's got snake eggs, Nicolas Nickolby and Batt Masterson yodeling, stormy seas, fleet footed indians, brutish mountain men, kissing and dancing but no monkeys.

*(These are from the time of the founding of **The Bystander**.)*

Who Am I? More and more it is being revealed to me that I haven't a clue. I have been thinking that this house will tell me part of it. On the list. entitled, Paths To The Solution there is: doesn't mind gardening.

I went to do some volunteer work, funny what my assignment was going to be: teach ex-cons how to spell. Some reading and writing but spelling loomed large in there. Imagine that. me, teaching spelling.

I'm reguarded as some sort of comedy outlaw who had better be careful of his next violation.

No longer aM I simply starting a magazine, I am founding a promise land. But every once in a while, the pendulum swings out the other way and I'll stand frozen staring out of a window my eyes spinning around in my head like those of an animated duck who has just been bashed over the noggon with a frying pan.

It's been real interesting. It's as if the baby has been born with a head that doesn't resemble any of the other babies' heads. A few people have rallied to it and say it's a good head. The others, in the majority, just don't know what to say.

It can really come true. Simply, it's going to be a place where talented people can show their work.

We did come from a land of girls and cats and this is a land of dogs and boys.

HANDEY & McCONNACHIE

The Dracula Letters

Dear Mr. Handey:
I saw your name in a pretty cosmopolitan magazine recently and you alluded to Count Dracula so I wanted to ask you, does the Count answer prayers like many of the undead who reside in heaven seem to? Some of the villagers who work at the coffin factory believe he does. If it's true, could you ask him how I can make some money? I'm all confused about how to make money. I'm not doing something right because guess what I don't have any of?

Thanks,
Brian McConnachie
and…
All Hail Count Dracula

Dear Mr. McConnachie:
Find a baby and give it to Dracula. That'll get you on his good side.
Then he'll cut you in on some deals.
All Hail Count Dracula,
Jack Handey

Dear Mr. Handey:
When you say "find a baby" do you mean, "steal a baby"? Or could you possibly mean, go and meet somebody nice, start taking them to dinner, fall in love, marry them and have a baby. And give the baby to Dracula. Which is a little more work than I was planning on, frankly.

I spent some time last week hanging around the village (the Village of the Coffin Makers) and they were saying The Count is still licking his wounds over the sub-prime house-flipping fiasco.

Have you heard otherwise?
Trying to get ahead,
Brian
All Hail Count Dracula

Dear Brian,
Yes, steal a baby. Or, if you have to, buy one. The count has a fondness for Swiss babies. But, to be honest, you can just get a baby doll and fill it full of blood. He won't know the difference.
The coffin makers are wrong. The count sold his castle at the peak of the market to Jack Nicholson.
All Hail Count Dracula!
Jack

Dear Jack:
Yes, the villagers said he's really near-sighted so the blood-filled doll might work.

I got a doll from a Swiss catalogue. (FYI They're not cheap. Euros! Cripes!) I'll fill it with a pint of my own blood. The directions are in French so I hope I'm doing this right. I think it's a kind of a "Betsy Wetsy"-type deal: You squeeze it and the liquid squirts out. But it squirts out a hole in the bottom. If he wants to bite the neck, the blood is just going to go all over his shoes. Unless he holds the baby doll up-side down. And THEN bites it.

Do I have to be there when he does this?
A.H.C.D.,
Brian

Dear Brian:
I know what you're saying about the doll. To be honest, I think it's actually easier to just steal someone's baby. Or buy one. You can get them online.
I'd be there when you give it to him. Otherwise his personal assistant Michelle will take credit for it.
A.H.C.D.,
Jack

Dear Jack:
I did both. I bought one AND I stole one. I also got a Paddington Bear and soaked it in cranberry juice. The babies are cute as the dickens. I can't tell them apart. But the Villagers from the Village of the Coffin Makers sure can! They've been chasing me around the village for the past day and a half. The good news is they never spread out — "…you go that way; you men go there and the rest, follow me!" — They hunt me in one big tight pack. Banging into each other and falling over each other. I yelled back at them, "Don't you guys have to go to work? And someone yelled back, "it's not our shift yet." Then I heard someone else say, "Don't talk to him. He's the Wolfman." I almost stopped in my tracks. The Wolfman! The hell you say. Anybody see hair growing on my ears?

I wanted to yell back, "I am not the Wolfman. I'm just a regular guy just doing what it takes to try and get ahead. And make some money. Live the dream." But that's a lot more than I could have gotten out after running around this screwy village for a day and a half with a baby in each arm plus a stuffed, juice-soaked bear. Then they'll change shifts on me. My only hope is that they really work them hard at the coffin factory.

I caught a break. Shift Two was exhausted. I made it up to the castle and got in. But then I looked around the reception area and Jeeez! What is this? Open baby night?!

There is no way he's going to see all these babies before the sun comes up.

What should I do? Leave and take my chances with the villagers? Or just jump the line?

FYI Michelle is off tonight. But she's back tomorrow. I don't want to deal with her.
A.H.C.D.,
Brian

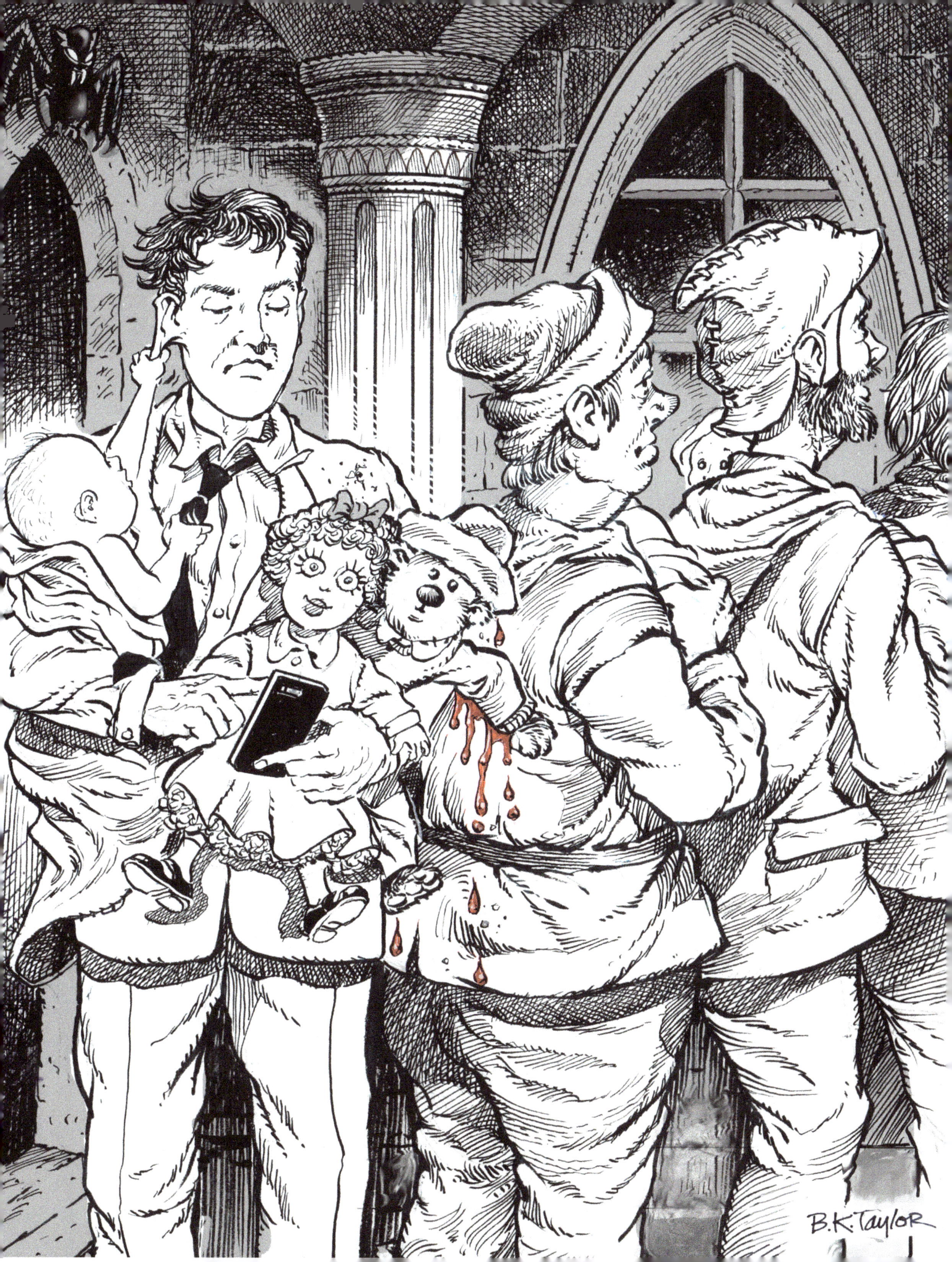
B.K. Taylor

REACH INBOX HERO

PLAY THE EPIC EMAIL GAME

ADVENTURE SNACK.com

A.H.C.D.,
Can you juggle? The count loves juggling. My plan depends on your ability to juggle three objects of unequal weight: the two babies and the bear. This will get His Majesty's attention.

Otherwise, I would suggest growling at the other people in line. Hopefully, someone will turn and yell, "IT'S THE WOLF MAN!!" Then they'll all run off.

I heard Michelle got a better offer from Dick Cheney, and she won't be around much longer. Let's hope.
A.H.C.D.,
Jack

I can juggle!

When I was in the Army, I'd go around to the veteran's hospitals whistling the William Tell Overture and juggle three tennis balls at once for all our boys in bed. But not three items of different weight. That was a little above my pay grade, as we used to say in the Army Infantry, USO, Juggling Division — "The Tossing Thirty-Fourth" — The Fe-Fi-Foes of Terror. And it was always the same three tennis balls. If you lost one, you'd be cleaning toilets for a month. Some of the guys preferred Indian clubs but I felt pretty comfortable with tennis balls.

So, yes, I know the principles of juggling.

I looked around the reception area with the frail hope of finding some tennis balls and saw a suit of armor that was holding a mace and chain. You know that big spiky ball attached to a chain and that's attached to a thick stick that you hold it with and swing it around your head? I'll just say, you'd hate to misjudge that one coming down back at you if you were juggling with it… wait! Forget the other two items, what about this? Just throwing the mace and chain in the air and trying to catch it. That could be dangerous-crazy-enough. He might like that. Would he like that? I'm not saying I could even do it but it's a thought.

What do you think?

"Gerald Beeman? Eighteen years ago you were driving through Connecticut and threw an apple out the window. The apple landed in a field alongside I-95 and…well…I think I'm your son."

Some guy just came down the big staircase with a real baffled look on his face and holding one totally drained baby by the ankle.

We asked. "What did he say? What did he say?"

He said, "Invent Velcro." A lot of people moaned at this.

Now in his defense, he might have been saying this since 1474 or however long he's been around and it was probably a good idea in its time. But it doesn't exactly apply these days. And how could you invent Velcro if you didn't know what it was? That's the part that really got us all scratching our heads. It's like Andrew Jackson telling the head of his Commerce Department to invent Mop & Glo. He'd go, "HUH?"

So we're all standing around asking this guy more questions about the Count when over the intercom comes a voice, I'm guessing, is the Count's. It's kind of Romanian-sounding.

"Can anyone out there juggle?" the voice asks. Boy! You called that one.

We all look around at each other. I'm about to speak up when I'm hit with some serious reality. Do I go in with the two babies and the juice soaked bear OR leave one baby and take the mace and chain? And try something I've never rehearsed. OR leave both babies and just go in with the mace and chain (hope for the best) and turn to one of these weirdoes in the reception area and say, "Excuse me. Would you please keep an eye on these babies for me?"

How did you know about the juggling? That's pretty inside stuff.

A.H.C.D.

A.H.C.D.,
My moneymaking job with the Count is to check out people who come to him for moneymaking ideas.

So that's how I know about your juggling. And your ability to talk like a robot for hours on end, even though people ask you to please stop.

I'd go with the babies and the bear, and I'll tell you why: CD has a cork floor in his office. I think the walls are cork too. He loves cork. So if you juggle the babies and drop them, no big deal. They're still pumping that baby blood.

A.H.C.D.

A.H.C.D. —
I think you're misunderstanding something. When people ask me to please stop talking like a robot, what they're saying, what they're DOING is getting "in character" with me and condemning the whole robot philosophy that I (as a pretend robot) am espousing. When they say, "... please stop saying that..." what they mean, I'm almost certain, is "please stop saying the robots will take over. It's mak-

THE VIRTUAL MEMORIES SHOW

In its 8th year, **The Virtual Memories Show** is a weekly podcast hosted by **Gil Roth,** featuring talks with writers, cartoonists, artists, musicians, and other creative types, including these **American Bystander** contributors:

RO Blechman • Barry Blitt • MK Brown
Roz Chast • Seymour Chwast
Joe Ciardiello • John Cuneo
Liza Donnelly • Bob Eckstein
Drew Friedman • Michael Gerber
Mort Gerberg • Sam Gross
Ben Katchor • Ken Krimstein
Peter Kuper • Merrill Markoe
Mimi Pond • Shannon Wheeler

As well as
Jules Feiffer • Ann Telnaes • Moby
Posy Simmonds • Chris Ware
Carol Tyler • Harold Bloom • Ed Ward
Milton Glaser • Molly Crabapple
Pete Bagge • Thomas Dolby • Kaz
Steven Heller • Barbara Nessim
Irvine Welsh, and 300+ more!

"If I've had a better interview, I don't remember it."
—Bruce Jay Friedman • *A Mother's Kisses*

"Gil Roth is a dream interviewer: relaxed, erudite, jaw-droppingly well-prepared, notably gracious in a graceless age."
—Mark Dery • *Born To Be Posthumous*

"He doesn't just ask questions, he wants to know where the answers lead. One of the best interviews I've ever had!"
—Kathe Koja •
Under The Poppy, The Cipher, and *Skin*

"A great, omnivorous interviewer on one of the most entertaining podcasts going."
—Peter Trachtenberg •
Another Insane Devotion

Find The Virtual Memories Show on iTunes & at vmspod.com

---

ing me scared." But in reality, they like to be scared. Doesn't everyone?

The first robot voice I did, and still my best, is Robbie when he warns Will Robinson about "the danger." People love it when I do that one. I can't do Hal from *2001* yet but I'm working on it.

Any-hoo, back to business. A couple of things. Two things. I should have mentioned this before but the Paddington Bear I soaked in cranberry juice is now covered with flies. And I'm pretty sure these babies need changing. I'm going to need a bottle of Clorox and a sink. Where does the Count keep his Clorox and is there a downstairs bathroom I can use? I just realized, "Clorox" sounds like a robot name. And there is a player on the Yankees called "Carlos Beltran". That's a robot name if I've ever heard one. I wonder just how many of our professional athletes have secret robot names? Probably a lot more than we'd like to think.

And secondly, does His Majesty speak and understand English?

That last guy to come out is now saying he *thinks* the Count said "Invent Velero." And I can't be certain it was the Count who said, "Can anyone out there juggle?" I'm assuming it was the Count, but maybe it was his translator.

I know actors who have played him speak and understand English but we're not talking about that because if they didn't, just think how slow the Dracula movies would wind up being with all the "What did he just say?" "…well you tell him this for me…" Then "…he said that, did he?…" And "…well, you can tell him he's not going to get away with it. Not this time." Also "…Now what's he saying?…I have to sleep in the basement! Ask him 'why there are no locks in these doors?' And on and on and on. See how slow that could get?

I think the second shift of villagers from the Village of the Coffin Makers are outside all banging on the door at once. Somebody's banging on the door. And they're angry.

And guess what just came up? The sun!

Please advise.

A.H.C.D.
Brian B

PARENT-TEACHER CONFERENCE

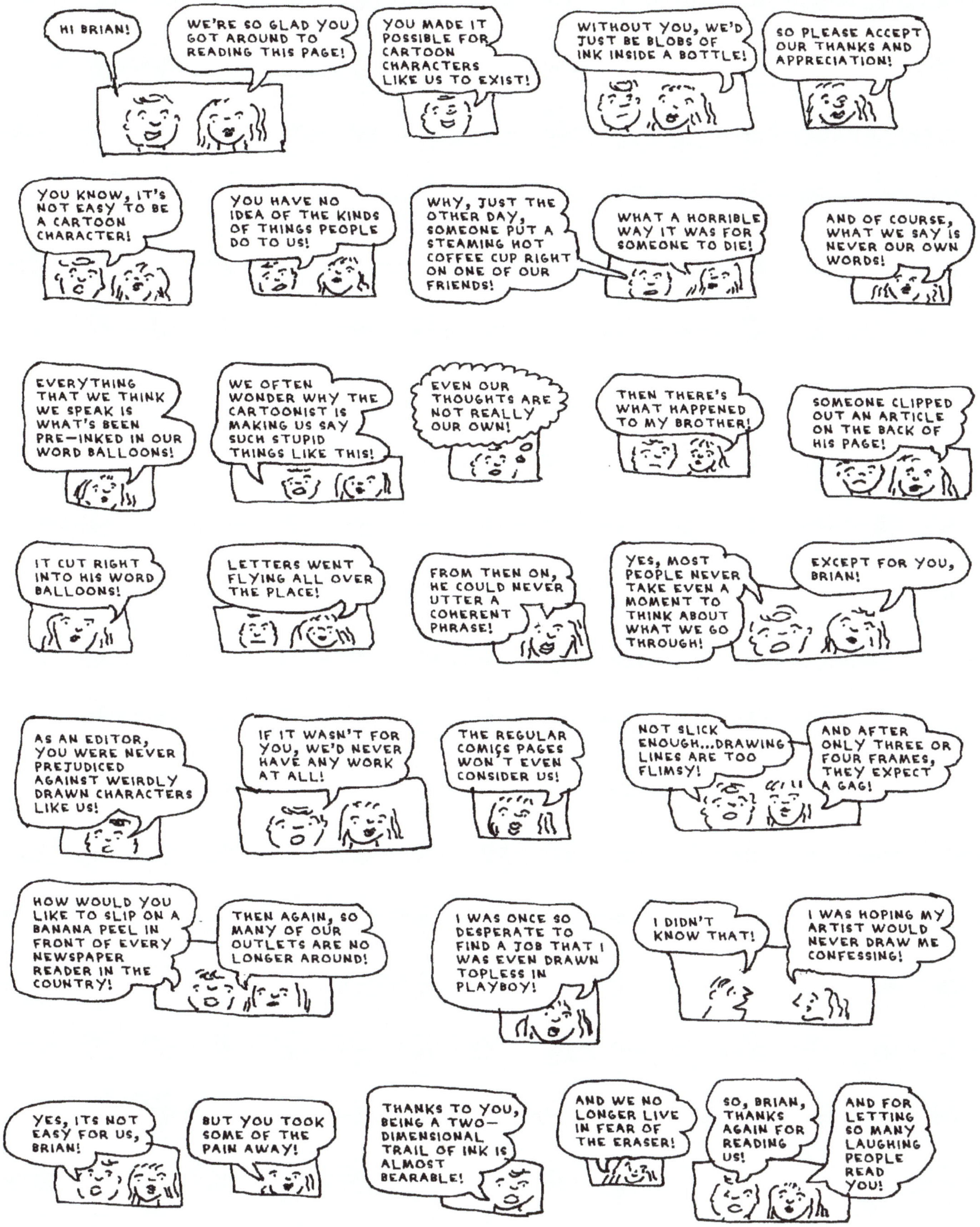
HI BRIAN!
WE'RE SO GLAD YOU GOT AROUND TO READING THIS PAGE!
YOU MADE IT POSSIBLE FOR CARTOON CHARACTERS LIKE US TO EXIST!
WITHOUT YOU, WE'D JUST BE BLOBS OF INK INSIDE A BOTTLE!
SO PLEASE ACCEPT OUR THANKS AND APPRECIATION!
YOU KNOW, IT'S NOT EASY TO BE A CARTOON CHARACTER!
YOU HAVE NO IDEA OF THE KINDS OF THINGS PEOPLE DO TO US!
WHY, JUST THE OTHER DAY, SOMEONE PUT A STEAMING HOT COFFEE CUP RIGHT ON ONE OF OUR FRIENDS!
WHAT A HORRIBLE WAY IT WAS FOR SOMEONE TO DIE!
AND OF COURSE, WHAT WE SAY IS NEVER OUR OWN WORDS!
EVERYTHING THAT WE THINK WE SPEAK IS WHAT'S BEEN PRE-INKED IN OUR WORD BALLOONS!
WE OFTEN WONDER WHY THE CARTOONIST IS MAKING US SAY SUCH STUPID THINGS LIKE THIS!
EVEN OUR THOUGHTS ARE NOT REALLY OUR OWN!
THEN THERE'S WHAT HAPPENED TO MY BROTHER!
SOMEONE CLIPPED OUT AN ARTICLE ON THE BACK OF HIS PAGE!
IT CUT RIGHT INTO HIS WORD BALLOONS!
LETTERS WENT FLYING ALL OVER THE PLACE!
FROM THEN ON, HE COULD NEVER UTTER A COHERENT PHRASE!
YES, MOST PEOPLE NEVER TAKE EVEN A MOMENT TO THINK ABOUT WHAT WE GO THROUGH!
EXCEPT FOR YOU, BRIAN!
AS AN EDITOR, YOU WERE NEVER PREJUDICED AGAINST WEIRDLY DRAWN CHARACTERS LIKE US!
IF IT WASN'T FOR YOU, WE'D NEVER HAVE ANY WORK AT ALL!
THE REGULAR COMICS PAGES WON'T EVEN CONSIDER US!
NOT SLICK ENOUGH...DRAWING LINES ARE TOO FLIMSY!
AND AFTER ONLY THREE OR FOUR FRAMES, THEY EXPECT A GAG!
HOW WOULD YOU LIKE TO SLIP ON A BANANA PEEL IN FRONT OF EVERY NEWSPAPER READER IN THE COUNTRY!
THEN AGAIN, SO MANY OF OUR OUTLETS ARE NO LONGER AROUND!
I WAS ONCE SO DESPERATE TO FIND A JOB THAT I WAS EVEN DRAWN TOPLESS IN PLAYBOY!
I DIDN'T KNOW THAT!
I WAS HOPING MY ARTIST WOULD NEVER DRAW ME CONFESSING!
YES, ITS NOT EASY FOR US, BRIAN!
BUT YOU TOOK SOME OF THE PAIN AWAY!
THANKS TO YOU, BEING A TWO-DIMENSIONAL TRAIL OF INK IS ALMOST BEARABLE!
AND WE NO LONGER LIVE IN FEAR OF THE ERASER!
SO, BRIAN, THANKS AGAIN FOR READING US!
AND FOR LETTING SO MANY LAUGHING PEOPLE READ YOU!

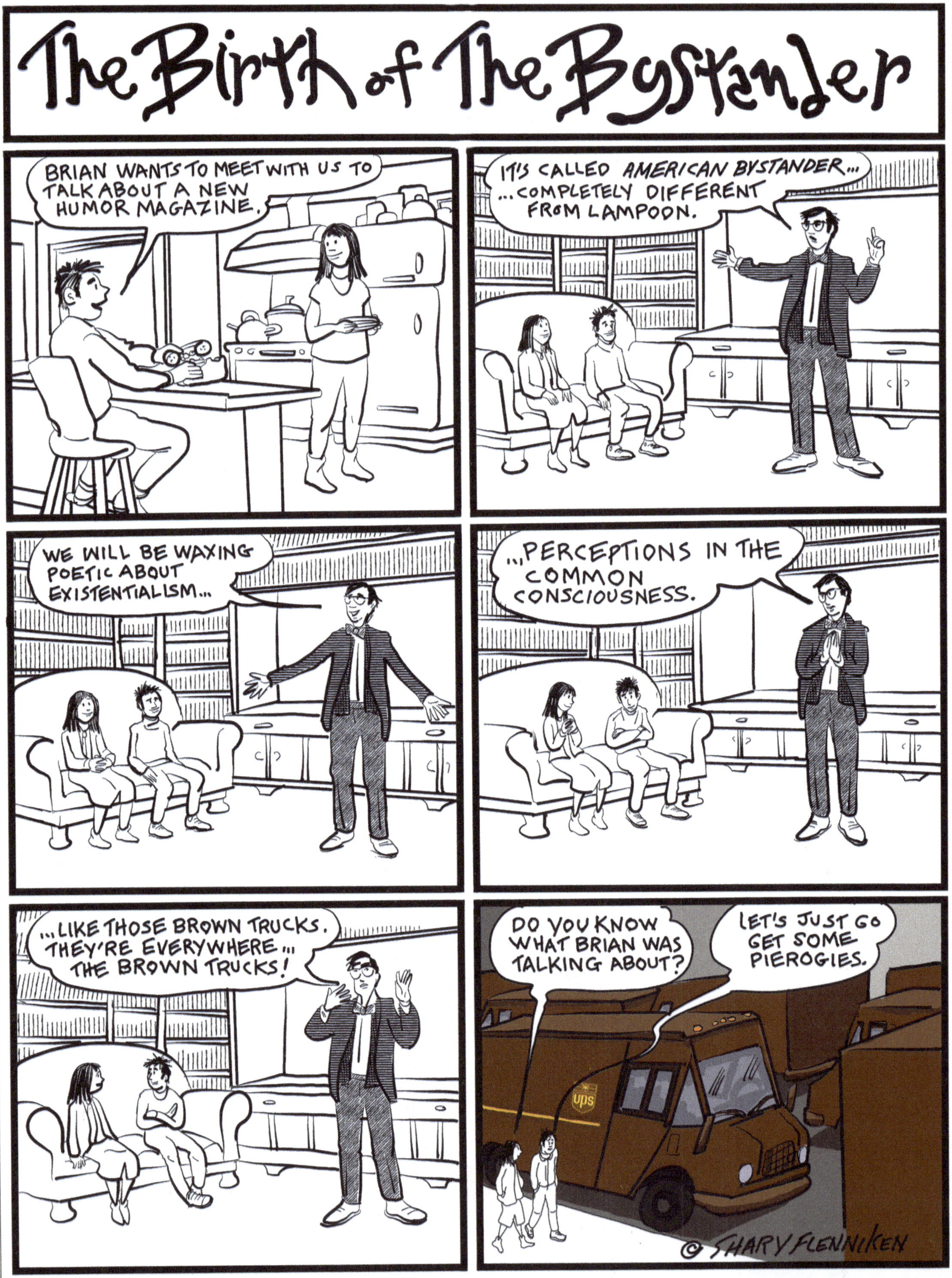
The Birth of The Bystander
BRIAN WANTS TO MEET WITH US TO TALK ABOUT A NEW HUMOR MAGAZINE.
IT'S CALLED *AMERICAN BYSTANDER*... ...COMPLETELY DIFFERENT FROM LAMPOON.
WE WILL BE WAXING POETIC ABOUT EXISTENTIALISM...
...PERCEPTIONS IN THE COMMON CONSCIOUSNESS.
...LIKE THOSE BROWN TRUCKS. THEY'RE EVERYWHERE... THE BROWN TRUCKS!
DO YOU KNOW WHAT BRIAN WAS TALKING ABOUT?
LET'S JUST GO GET SOME PIEROGIES.
UPS
© SHARY FLENNIKEN

Baseball Is Hunting

When I drive that section of dirt road to and from work, there are often robins or swallows or crows standing or sitting in the road. As I approach, they scatter though some cut it pretty close. First disappearing under the car, seeming to be goners but then miraculously emerging, like the Blue Angels, banking off to the left and right.

It could be older birds training younger ones how to judge distance, mass and velocity and then put it all to the test. Admiring their skill and wanting to be helpful, I keep my speed at a constant 10 M.P.H. when I drive at them. (If this is what they're doing—I've quit watching the nature shows on public television at the insistence of Walter Wells, a former neighbor, who convinced me that they make it all up to match the amazing footage they've amassed over the years.) I've also considered the birds could just be pecking at the dirt, hoping for a worm or two, confident in their ability to scram when necessary.

But once beyond this stretch, when it turns into asphalt, my thoughts on their Ranger-camp bird-skills depart my mind, leaving my current thoughts mostly in the possession of Victoria Wells, former wife of said Walter, who both moved away some five years ago. My own ex had departed the region just before the Wells's had arrived. But now Victoria may have returned, which if true, is of disturbing concern to me. I believed I was over her but now can't stop thinking it was her I saw buying gas the other night.

I was stopped at a light while driving home from a meeting at the VFW hall populated by parents and parent/coaches who were considering a plan to extend the town's Little League season from July 4th through Labor Day.

Most parents who coach usually have a child on the team they coach. I'm not a parent and probably for that reason some parents have been urging me, and a few other childless locals, to please get involved. They want more impartiality and a less competitive atmosphere; they want an atmosphere where everyone cheerfully roots for everyone else.

The league's regular season ended on a disturbing note with a parent, from the visitor's side, muttering louder and louder; then he trotted out to the pitcher's mound, where his son had just walked in two runs, losing the lead. The boy's father started shouting.

"Okay, you wanted my attention, you got it. So let's get it out. Just what are you trying to do here? Disgrace me? Because that's exactly what you're doing and you damn well know it. Just wait till I get you home, pal—NO! You get this next batter out or you just better not plan on coming home!"

Not wanting to give this incident more attention than it caused, the episode was thereafter referred to as "that thing that happened with the guy." It was first used as an argument for *not* extending the season, suggesting we leave this business behind and start fresh again in the spring with some new rules in place. But a growing majority—a number of whom were at the game in question and so regretted their own inaction—now believed that by extending the season they would not be bending to that behavior. They would bury that thing that happened with the guy under an extended season of dreamy afternoons, cherishing noncompetitive baseball games and nearby dappled sunlight.

Through the paused traffic and gas pumps, I saw only part of a woman's back but knew it was her. Her name had come up a few times lately. I'd heard she and Walter divorced. I was sorry about that. In spite of what my intentions toward her ultimately were, I always believed she and Walter had a beguiling relationship that co-authored some spirited battles of enviable passion.

I should have pulled in behind her, but was stuck in the outside lane with cars honking for me to move it. Also, we hadn't parted on the best of terms: indifference on her part and feigned indifference on mine. If someone had a question with her as some, or all, of the answer, I'd retreat behind a bewildered stare.

"Matt! What's her name? You know who I mean. Curly hair, over the top, perky. Always in motion. Flirts well with others. Married to that tall guy, the doper. He's a chemist for some big food corporation. C'mon. She was a tennis instructor. You know who I'm talking about —"

"Uuummm...No. I really don't...I don't, really." My passion for her made me self conscious, as I attempted to conceal all interest I held for everything remotely connected to her.

"Well guess what? I think she's moved back."

I had already become friends with Walter before I had met her. He had a range of odd interests and a playful feminine side. He'd drop by occasionally. We'd smoke a little dope that he'd provide, put on some tunes and speculate about lives lived at the edge of an expanding universe. He worked for General Foods but wouldn't say what he did there, which became a running joke.

"I make sure the frozen peas are frozen at the exact, right moment. 'The moment of readiness,' we like to call it," he'd say with a wink. Occasionally he'd bring up his buddy, Vic, mentioning trips they've taken together; but until I met Vic I had assumed Vic was male. When I did meet her and her tomboy nature, I saw their snug synchronization.

Sitting on the porch, Walter and I would let the conversation drift until it bumped into something we'd both enjoy contributing to.

"I was reading about the earliest Phoenicians where the children's toys had wheels on them, but the adults were still dragging rocks around in a net of ropes."

"When they finally straightened that out, did they acknowledge the kids with a holiday?" I asked.

"I think they were too embarrassed. But it freed them up to start working on their precious alphabet that they made the kids stay indoors memorizing on lovely Mediterranean afternoons."

"Were there other things the kids were keeping from their betters?" I said.

"Oh, yes."

"Like what? Frozen foods?" I said.

"Frozen foods, yes…that would definitely be one," Walter said. "We still use their secret formula, you know."

This idea—learning from play, "The child is father to the man"—stuck with me. It then joined up with another major ponderable, baseball. That's when I realized something so fundamental about baseball: Baseball is hunting. It's hunting as a game that has almost perfectly evolved. All the men in the field are traps. The pitcher is the hunter with the powerful, accurate arm. The catcher

helps flush out the prey. The batter, the bunny rabbit, or whatever, has to get from one safe place to the next. The traps are set. Then the pitcher/hunter sets it all in motion. Everybody gets to be the traps and everyone gets to be the bunny. Except in the DH-corrupted American League version.

I thought Walter might get a kick out of this so I dropped in for a visit. My first to his house. We sat on the back porch and talked about the childhood influences that transcend our lives. Building to the reveal, I wanted to give the idea a modest preamble. "I was thinking," I began, "that probably all sports no matter what objective they have could be training for a particular function in later life. Such as, football is war. The soldiers capturing territory. Attacking, defending. And rugby is similar. I think. Not altogether sure about rugby. Running off with a big leather egg filled with milk chocolate? The spoils of war? It appears to be a rough struggle, so let's for the sake of war call it war.

"Then there are those contests that Red Smith called 'the back and forth sports': lacrosse, soccer, basketball, hockey, polo, water polo, which is a half of a back and forth sport. All those could be various"—I was reaching here—"sales positions?"

"Where are you putting tennis and all its paddle-wielding offspring like squash, ping-pong, badminton and racquetball?" he asked.

"Tennis is probably boxing at a safe distance. Actually, you could put it in with war; the artillery division. But we're getting off-track here. The rest are mostly individual achievement. Track and field, swimming, golf, horse racing," I said. "But of all sports, the most difficult, sophisticated, evolved, complex, elegant and violent, and the one that stands unique"—here I lowered my voice and raised my brows—"is baseball. Baseball is hunting. What is more ancient and universal than hunting?"

Walter thought for a while. "Then what is hunting?" he said. "I'm not sure I'm with you on this."

"Are you a baseball fan?" I said.

"Not really."

"Are you a sports fan?"

"I like tennis," he said. "I like the outfits."

Since it was new, I went slowly. There were certainly flaws but this day's version would merely introduce the overall thesis. Later, I'd do the polish.

"Think of all the players on the field as traps," I told Walter, as I heard someone inside the house. "It requires every bit of a man's instinct, knowledge, speed and strength. It's quiet, it's still, then—BAM! It explodes into orchestrated chaos that can happen so fast, a dozen things can go on at once..."

The door opened and out came a woman dressed in shorts and a green T-shirt with an emblem of crossed tennis racquets on it.

"Hey babe," she said.

"Hey babe," Walter said. "Didn't hear you drive in."

"Hell-o, there. Is this your imaginary friend? It's Matt, right? Hi. Good to finally meet you and see you exist. Walter has been telling me about you. I'm the wifie, Victoria."

She came towards me. I rose, and staring at her, mostly missed her extended hand but we caught and pinched the tips of each other's fingers.

"What are you guys up to?"

"I was just saying to Walter—"

"Matt? Has someone offered you a drink? You don't have a drink. Let me get you something. Today's Friday. That's a gin day for me. I'm going to have gin and tonic. In fact, I think it's all we have," she said adding, "Did you get to the store today, babe?"

"I asked him if he wanted a drink, babe. He said he didn't. Didn't I ask you? I'm not totally worthless as a host, am I?" said Walter. "But I did go to the store."

"I'm fine, really," I said. Thank you."

"You sure? The train's leaving. It's the gin-town express. Yes? No? What are you guys talking about?" she said, heading back into the house.

"Matt thinks baseball is an ancient endeavor. Like hunting," Walter answered.

"I knew it was prehensile," she said.

"Keep talking but louder so I can hear you. But please, not about baseball. OK?"

She then told a story, out the kitchen window, in considerable detail, about her father taking her to a baseball game and how she didn't like a minute of it. She preferred football or tennis. I thought, what a shame because she'd look great in a baseball cap, a ponytail bouncing out the back as she wildly cheered the runner rounding third. Then she brought up tennis, and I never got any further with my baseball-as-hunting thesis.

As nice as it was to have such an attractive and friendly neighbor, I initially kept my distance. I found Vic would interrupt the interesting to rephrase

the obvious. Or she would monopolize a conversation she had interrupted by offering what she didn't know about a topic that was no longer being discussed because she had shoved it onto a corner and blocked anyone who would try to retrieve it for the better common interest. She was quick and proficient at this. And I found her to be randomly short-tempered and intolerant of Walter when he tried to cure her of this. Occasionally she'd fire back a "Shut up!" that felt as hurtful as a slap across the face. But then, like the electricity suddenly going back on, she'd resume talking as if hadn't happened.

So for a while, whenever I saw Vic approaching, like a child needing to hide favorite toys from a reckless sibling, I'd quickly wrap up my end of a conversation with Walter and be on my way.

Traditionally many families headed off during July or August. But this year fewer families had those plans and that meant there were more than enough kids to populate six teams.

The games were seven innings long. The coaches, there were at least two, would pitch to his or her own team for the first three innings. When the coaches pitched to their own team, strikes counted but balls did not and a team could only bat around once.

I become a co-coach for the Dodgers with Peter Kloit who manages the dairy department at the Shopwellrandom. Mostly, he worked with pitching and batting.

Among our notable players was the barrel-chested Gino Salvatore, who only liked batting. To him, fielding was like cleaning your room—for wussies. He would plant himself in the outfield like a teamster with his arms intractably folded across his chest. A ball would practically have to roll over his foot—with parents, coaches and teammates screaming at him—before he'd pick it up and lob it to the cutoff man.

There was Sean Delaney, at second base, a thin child with the efficient bony framework of a potential marathon runner. He was the only boy among four older sisters all known for their dexterity at Irish step dancing. At second, he'd often be on his toes, hopping from foot to foot, in constant motion as if keeping time with the fiddles, flutes and war drums that were unceasingly banging away in his head.

There were the twins, Andy and Paul Brewer, who played first and shortstop respectively—and were good at it. They also pitched. A&P were handsome and inseparable and full of grandmotherly advice for their teammates on matters of personal hygiene, traffic crossings and the value of chewing food throughly. They were the team's biggest boosters who wept dramatically when we lost and went leaping, into deranged paroxysms of joy whenever we won. (Which was about half the time.)

At third base was Zed Krouse, who had the most natural talent, but only a casual interest. Zed would sometimes

THE NEW NORMAL

play barefoot and wear his mitt on his head and stand with his hands in his pockets and his back to the plate looking off at whatever else he found more interesting—which might be anything else other than the game he was playing. Zed had a growing artistic temperament. Somedays he'd put in a great effort and other days not. We let him be. Coach Kloit and I agreed he was a good example of "picking your fights."

Behind the plate was George Weigel, who had the bulk and fearlessness that suggested a real future as a catcher. He mumbled a fair amount. I suspected it was an inaudible narrative of the game currently underway; could he be eye-ing a broadcasting career if the catching didn't pan out?

Being raised indifferently by a single mom was Clifford Blake. Young Clifford.

Master Blake. He was a plumpish boy of privilege with soft cherubic looks and curly black hair who had no instincts for, or interest in, this confounding, dangerous and pointless activity that his mother had thoughtlessly sentenced him to. Clifford had a small plastic mitt that more resembled a yellowing hand infection than standard baseball equipment. He held this gently over his heart and then over his face whenever the *ping* of a bat and shouting announced the ball was in play and possibly en route, determined to hit him in some soft, unprotected place where the sting of pain lingers far longer than the laws of physics should mercifully allow. But Clifford was the most obliging boy on the team. He tried with all effort to do everything I asked of him, while his sad, wide eyes searched for the hope that

Life will go on, and all the perils of hardball would one day be safely inert in his diary. Then he would at last be able to joke about the ordeal—as he'd heard a number of self-deprecating adults often do on various subjects as he, dressed in a child's tuxedo, served them warm *hors d'oeuvres* at one of his mother's popular cocktail parties. Though Clifford's bad habits were deep, and his fear of the ball deeper still, he did improve. His willingness to persevere made me admire him more than anyone else on the team. Initially, Clifford would get out of the way of the ball, and when it bounced safely past him, he'd give chase. Yelling at it to stop, he'd throw his mitt at it—which was swiftly followed by the realization he valued his mitt more than he wanted the ball, thus redirecting his pursuit. His mistakes and their solutions kept him one busy boy in the outfield.

It was during our fourth game that Clifford caught a ball. It was a high fly he was simultaneously trying to get nearer to and away from, but in doing so, found himself directly under. For a moment the ball appeared wedged between his neck and shoulder. Then, like a wandering goiter seeking toasty sanctuary in the depths of Clifford's underwear, it vanished.

"Don't move!" his teammates yelled.

The umpire gave it a fair amount of time to reappear out his pant's leg and thump to the ground. When it did not, he called the batter out and a cheer went up, "Clif-*ford*! Clif-*ford*!"

Over a short amount of time, my objections to Victoria grew inconsequential. I didn't care if she talked too much about nothing, she was fun to be around. The three of us were spending more healthy weekend time together, hiking, kayaking and sailing on Shepard's Lake. Then came the evening when the climate between us changed, or so I believed.

She had invited me for supper with another couple. While shaving and thinking about what I'd wear, I realized how much my vanity had been aroused, and how I looked forward to seeing her and absorbing her possessive, welcoming hug.

Their porch chairs were lined up facing west. We sat on the deck with our drinks watching the sun, like a golden coin, deposit itself into the back hills of Massachusetts—while opposite, keeping the balance, a creamy, pumpkin moon ascended. We talked about the errors of the Town Board compounded by the Zoning Board. Then about the exploding deer population, and the ever-escalating cost of coyote urine and their even more costly and foul derivatives.

As Victoria placed a refill next to me, she ran her hand across my shoulders igniting a fuse that sent something utopian up my spine. Without turning, I reached around to pat her hand just as she removed it, leaving me patting myself.

During dinner, I told a story about a raccoon chasing me. It made her laugh. She jumped up from her seat and gave me a hug and a kiss on the cheek. I looked at Walter as he was lowering his head.

At the door, saying our good nights, there was a brief but lip-y good night kiss between us. As I was getting into my car, Betsy, the other woman, said as she walked by, "Be careful, she's a cat."

Walter also cautioned me. "It's not what you think. Don't misunderstand her. People sometimes believe her affection is for them. It's not directed at anyone in particular. It's her nature. It's for everybody. Men, women, children, dogs, trees and plants. Everyone but cats. To think it's more personal is a mistake. She doesn't have many women friends; only Betsy, which is regrettable. But she tries."

Among the fundamentals, concentration came first. We called it the 'The Big C.'

"What do we need?"

"The big C!"

"When do we need it?"

"Now!"

The first time we yelled this, just before a game, the opposing coach came over. He told me his wife was undergoing chemo, so would we not chant that?

"Sorry about your wife," I told him. I hadn't thought about the other big "C." I made a note to come up with another chant. And a second note to explain to the boys that baseball is hunting which maybe could give them an edge. If they never win another game, they'll always have that.

Then I remembered Arthur Miller's famous line: *Attention must be paid.* There were two ways to go with this: "What did Linda Loman say?" Or, "What did Mrs. Willy Loman say?"

We went with the latter.

I'd set them up and they'd shout, "Attention must be paid!"

"When must it be paid?" I'd yell.

"Now it shall be paid," they'd scream in a voice of wild boyhood, then bit off a *"YEAH!"* to seal the deal.

It was lumpy at first, but it smoothed out with repetition. I can't really say why, but I liked that our team was further distinguished by a theatrical reference to *Death of a Salesman*.

That opposing coach, the same one who objected to our earlier chant, came over and wanted to know what this new one was about. Since our last game, I'd learned his wife had only had a small "c"—a basal cell carcinoma removed at her doctor's office, a minor procedure.

Now this coach wanted to know "who this Mrs. Willy Loman is." He was like a cop slowly gathering evidence. I was about to tell him when I thought, no, if I told him, he'd find other objections. Willy Loman, for one. Things aren't going well for Mr. Willy Loman, so what does he do? He offs himself. Is that the message we want our Little Leaguers to carry into their promising futures?

Fundamentally, I think he just didn't like us having an unregulated chant, one he didn't get to pass official judgment on.

"So, who's this Mrs. Willy Loman?"

I told him Mrs. Loman recently donated a new research wing to the county hospital, and we were giving her a shout-out as we do at the start of our games to all who advance medical research. I know it'll come back to bite me.

The last time I tried to passionately explain my baseball-is-hunting theory was to Victoria. I wanted to bring her over to the enlightened side; I *knew* she could appreciate it.

Driving by one fine day, I saw who I believed to be Walter lounging out on the back porch. It was Vic, who never lounged anywhere—and was wearing a powerful bikini. I had never before seen her so undressed. The clothes she usually wore were always sizes too large. I was almost giddy by this figure she'd been concealing, a tummy that begged to be petted and stroked.

"Hey," I said. "Didn't realize it was

European Birdbath

you back here."

"Hey Matt. How have you been? I'm knocked out. I hit the wall. I'm calling it quits for the day," she said. "I'm just going to lie here and do nothing. What are you up to?"

"Um, not much. I just thought I'd say, hi and oh, I'm glad you're here. I just remembered something I really wanted to do..."

I really wanted to start kissing her stomach. And toss in a mess of zerberts as well. Get her laughing and wiggling and begging I stop.

"I never finished telling you my baseball is hunting theory ..."

"That's right. You like baseball, don't you?"

"I'm sure if you understood it you'd really enjoy it."

"You go ahead and tell me about your baseball. I'm all yours."

"Baseball is chess and everything else is checkers! No truer words," I said.

"My father taught me how to play chess. We ought to play one day. Okay, lay it on me," she said shutting her eyes.

"Well, baseball is hunting," I began.

"As in hunters and gatherers?"

"No. It's only about the hunters. I suppose there are gatherers like bat boys, ticket takers, vendors and such—but they don't affect the outcome."

"So what happened to the gatherers? Did the hunters run them off? I want to learn this," Vic said, stifling a yawn.

"Let me start again."

It took only a short while for her to get deep inside me, but years for her to grow out—if that's even happened. This was not something I pursued. It just happened. She reminded me of my first teen love; she had the same exuberance. On top of that, Vic strongly resembled my ex-, and—dear God—she had the same birthday as my mother!

She was the last thought I'd have at night, and the first one impatiently waiting for me in the morning—waiting to offer me more impetuous advice I should employ to speed along my misplaced passion and crash it into something nearby.

I would dwell upon her flaws and carry them around like buckets of ice water to douse myself with, but they

Hiking Trail Masking Fails by ER Flynn

A RECENT HIKE IN A WASHINGTON STATE PARK SHOWED ME WHY THE USA WILL BE *FOREVER TRAPPED* IN A SPIRAL OF *PANDEMIC LUNACY*.

WHILE WASHINGTON STATE HAS MANDATED THAT ALL PEOPLE WEAR MASKS TO HELP PREVENT THE TRANSMISSION OF COVID-19 MANY PEOPLE HAVE...UM... NOT REALLY GOTTEN THE HANG OF IT. HERE'S A FEW EXAMPLES OF MASKING GENIUS SPIED ALONG THE TRAIL...

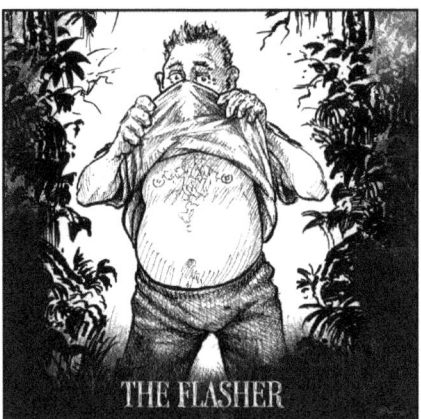

THE FLASHER – THINKS A SWEATY T-SHIRT AND BELLY FAT PROVIDES PROTECTION AGAINST DISEASE.

THE BELA LUGOSI – AN ARM HELD FIRMLY AGAINST ONE'S FACE PROVIDES PROTECTION...UNLESS THAT ARM HAS BEEN EXPOSED TO THE VIRUS... BLAH!

THE CHIN HAMMOCK – IT MAY NOT OFFER PROTECTION FROM CONTAGIONS BUT IS GREAT AT HIDING UNSIGHTLY CHIN FAT!

THE PROBLEMATIC PROBOSCIS – EXCELLENT, IF ONE'S NOSE IS ONLY USED TO HOLD UP GLASSES AND STORE NOSE HAIR!

THE EMPEROR'S NEW MASK – USUALLY SEEN NOT ONLY SPREADING DISEASE BUT ALSO DISCARDING TRASH ALONG THE TRAIL. IF THEY HAD THEIR CHOICE THEY'D DRIVE A "BRO-DOZER" SUPER TRUCK ON THE *TRAIL INSTEAD*.

THE COVID CAMO – THINKS VIRUSES CAN BE EASILY FOOLED AND WILL MOVE ON.

...NOW IF ONLY WE COULD.

wouldn't take. I could only find delight and more excitement in them that made the pain more torturous.

I dreamed about Victoria. I was in an art class and she was to be the figure model. Upon hearing that, I pushed my way to the front to set up my easel right next to where she'd be posing. But then realized this looked a bit lecherous. I began retreating a little further back. Then a little more. And a little more. Then it was too far. I was at the back wall and everyone else filled in. It was crowded. Then a big, "Ooooooo!" went up and I couldn't see a goddamn thing. I did hear her laughing and flirting with the guys up front and enjoying herself as much as they were.

One afternoon as I entering the park, I started thinking of places where I'd most likely run into her. I wondered if I should frequent some of those places when I heard someone behind me, and felt a hand slip into mine. It was Clifford. It felt most awkward and pleasant.

Last week there was a chocolate layer cake left on my porch. It looked like a child had made it or it had been dropped. The note read: "Thank you for helping Clifford. You've done heaps for his confidence, signed, Connie B. P.S. Cocktails and Dancing. Friday the 16th. 7 P.M. Hope you can come." It was my first invite to her legendary home.

"We have to concentrate more. Right, coach?" Clifford said, nodding emphatically.

"Why don't you run on ahead and get some more practice in?" He started away then paused. "What is it, son?"

"I was wondering before: do hippopotamuses think rhinos are unicorns?" Clifford smiled.

"Go on now," I said.

"Maybe it's where they got the *idea* for unicorns."

As I watched Clifford run off to engage in the unique seriousness of baseball, I resumed guessing where I might run into Victoria and what I'd say when it happened. "Hey! I think I know this guy," might work. But—it shouldn't be rehearsed.

For the most part, Peter Kloit was the hitting and pitching coach (I was the fielding coach). Most of the kids had trouble getting around on Peter's pitches; he'd throw fast. But that meant when they did get ahold of one, they took it for a ride.

On this day I noticed the other team was slow to show up. I thought it might be a good time to have a talk with our guys.

I called the team in. We all took a knee.

"I want to tell you something important about baseball that not many people know. Gather around. Can you all hear me? This might help you see the game more clearly. It might make you better players.

"When the other team is up and we're out in the field," I continued, "do you ever think about who you are?"

"...We're the...Dodgers?" someone offered.

"Anything else?"

They looked at each other for clues. Then a smile lit Clifford's face.

"We're Mrs. Willy Loman!" he shouted. A few more voices meekly endorsed this odd but reasonable response.

"No," I said. "When you're out there in the field, you're all *traps*, set to catch the batter. The batter has to run through the traps. Like a bunny. And you're the bunny-hunters. You're the traps that catch the bunny. Because baseball, when all is said and done, is hunting!"

"What kind of traps?" someone asked. "Like bear traps?"

"Don't get hung up on the traps. Don't get literal on me," I told them. "You can't let anyone get by you and get safely on base."

"Are the bases traps?" said Gino.

"What's 'literal' mean?" someone asked.

"Did somebody do something to the bases?" Gino asked Zed.

"Listen," I said. "It doesn't matter what kind of traps. What is important is that you know baseball is hunting," I said, "and we're going hunting."

"Coach, are we going to need permission slips?" asked one of the twins. "If you want, we can help collect them," said the other.

"I know! I know!" said Sean. "Can we be those traps where you dig a big hole, cover it over with twigs and leaves, and put spikes in the bottom?"

"Yeah! That's so cool." A few of the boys did imitations of being impaled on wooden spikes trying to stretch a single

---

"Stan Mack shows that a man can be as caretaking as a woman, and a woman can be as brave, funny, and loving in death as in life. This compassionate, irresistible memoir is a gift to all of us."
Gloria Steinem, author, *Moving Beyond Words*

JANET & ME

An Illustrated Story of Love and Loss by
STAN MACK

Available now
at Amazon, Powell's
or at your local booksellers.

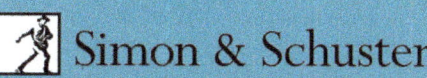
Simon & Schuster

"I THINK FOR OUR GENERATION THE AMERICAN DREAM IS TO GET OUT OF AMERICA."

into a double while twitching to death.

"Guys. Stop!"

"What about Have-A-Heart traps?" said Zed. "We have some in our garage. I don't think a person can fit in one."

"We'll try this later," I said. Coach Kliot stepped in and gave out the batting order and some tips for today's game.

I joined the procession of cars that stretched for almost a quarter of a mile, to a cleared field where teenagers in black pants and white shirts directed the parking. I'd been here once before as a tourist, but not as a guest. I'd heard for tax reasons the house is open to the public four days a year. (It's also available for non-profit events.) The house, which is on the National Registry, is a twenty-room American Gothic mansion built around 1850 by a prominent D.C. architect, and sits on about a hundred acres. The current owner, Connie Blake, got it in a divorce settlement.

There was a bar setup halfway between the parking field and the house. I got myself a drink, then looked around for someone to talk with. There were no faces I recognized. I went in the house and took a meandering tour of the first floor and spotted Peter Kloit and his wife, Pam, who appeared momentarily trapped in the butler's pantry where the caterers were storing boxes of food and liquor.

"Hi, you two," I said.

"Hey, Matt, how are you?" he said. "You know Pam."

"Hi, Pam. I think if you can climb over that carton you can come out this way."

"Wow. Some joint, huh?" Peter said.

"It's amazing," Pam said. "Imagine taking care of a place this size. Just cleaning part of the downstairs would take a week. Does she and the boy live here by themselves?"

"I think there's also an older daughter from an earlier marriage," I said.

"Hey, you'd never guess what happened. There was a chocolate cake at our door with a note inviting us here," Peter said.

"How about that," I said.

"It was good," he said.

We headed out on the veranda where there was live music and two more bars. It felt like a grand wedding. Swing standards were playing softly. A number of women were dancing with children and each other.

"Which one is Connie Blake? Do you know? I have to thank her for inviting us," said Pam, "and tell her how great her house is."

"I'd heard she doesn't make an appearance at her parties until they're well under way," I said. "Two or three hours in."

Peter piped up. "Matt, before I forget, I'm not going to be able to make our game tomorrow. Can you handle it by yourself? I've got some family business to deal with. Sorry to do this to you."

"No problem." I welcomed it.

I was watching the dancers and then saw young Clifford, in his tux, serving *hors d'oeuvres* to a group of people at the edge of the dance floor. And there among them, at last, was Victoria. She took a *hors d'oeuvre* from Clifford's tray, made a fuss over him, and gave him a long affectionate hug.

I crossed the floor and came up behind her as she turned around. She was almost expressionless but then she grabbed my belt buckle and shook me with it. Then smiled.

In all the time Victoria was married to Walter, she never once wore make-up—but this evening, she was in full war paint. She was hunting. It suited her.

"I think I know this guy. Hi there, you," she said. "I was wondering when we'd run into each other. Actually I saw you a few times in town but decided to leave it alone."

"Really? Why is that?"

"I was probably in a hurry," she said.

"Well, tell me what you've been up to," I said.

"Well, to begin with, I'm leaving tomorrow evening. For England. For a month. Can you believe that? But I'll tell you what, meet me tomorrow at the slip on Shepard's Lake. Two o'clock. In the boathouse. We'll steal some quality time together. We deserve it, don't you think? Maybe even take a swim."

"...Okay," I said.

"Sorry I can't talk now. I need to get back. I'm actually working here. Long story, but I'll see you tomorrow."

As I watched her leave, I was suddenly empty of any reason to stay. I headed home, head packed with her. She wants to meet me at Shepard's Lake, which means she wants to be alone with me. I dwelled on that for a while.

It wasn't until I got home that I realized the Dodgers had a game tomorrow and Peter would be away. Two o'clock would be cutting it close. If we start right at noon and finish by two, I wouldn't be that late.

I arrived early, and for a half hour was the only one there. The Dodgers were slow showing up. By the scheduled start of the game, I had half a team; we didn't have enough players.

There was nothing to do then but postpone or forfeit. Pick another day. The umpire gave us another fifteen minutes. Just when that time was up, two SUVs arrived with the rest of the Dodgers and some parents.

George, our catcher, came over. "Hey, Coach! I told my Dad what you said, that baseball was hunting, and he said he liked that idea. He'd like to talk to you about it. My dad loves baseball. This is the first game he's been able to come to. I'll go get him..."

"We've got to get going here, George..." I said weakly, but George ran off. He returned with a man in bright pants, a white shirt and golf shoes.

"Jeff Weigel." He extended his hand. "Never heard that before but yes, hunting, it makes sense. You've been giving this some thought, I suspect—"

"Nice to meet you, Jeff." I began backing away.

"Hold on, there's Mort—you've got to talk to this guy. *Mort!* He's a real fan. A stats guy. I want to see his reaction. Do you mind? Mort, get over here. You got to meet Coach and hear this," said Jeff.

"Jeff, I have some stuff to do..."

"Wont take a minute. Hey, did you read that Willy Mays bio? *Mort!* You're holding Coach up. Here he comes..."

"Sorry, hi," said Mort.

"He's a real fan. Tell him what you said about baseball is hunting. Tell him what you mean by that. He'll get a kick out of it. Mort, listen to this guy. He knows the inside."

"Well, baseball is hunting and...all the players on the field are traps...all the traps get set before each pitch..." I said.

"I like the sound of that. I'd love to hear more," said Mort.

"Guys..." I began.

"Okay, you're in a hurry. But after the game let's talk about this. We're not going to let you get away," said Jeff.

For the first time, I had the team to myself. When the kids saw me take the mound, they cheered. I was the coach who threw the fat lazy grapefruits, not the hard stuff. Everyone on the team, including Clifford, could wallop what I threw.

"Hooray for Coach!"

"We all bat around!"

"Big inning, everybody!"

"Get ready to do some damage, guys," I yelled. "We're gonna move this along."

First up was Zed. I held the ball up and away so he could get a good fix on it. I looked like I was throwing darts. The first pitch was wide; Zed chased it and missed. The next was inside and made him jump back. "Good

Explore the world's largest cartoon database

Over **500,000** cartoons from the **Bystander, New Yorker** & more

eye, good eye," his teammates cheered.

The next pitch was right at Zed, and as he jumped away, the ball hit his bat and dribbled down the third base line. He ran safely to first.

Andy was up next and the ball hit him in the shoulder as he twisted around to get away from it. The next pitch went at his head and bounced off his helmet. The next bounced in front of the plate and hit him in the ankle as he tried to jump over it. After dodging the next one, he swung and hit a ball a foot over his head for a single. Men on first and third.

I had never thrown so poorly. I had to concentrate.

I hit Sean in the thigh and the arm. I hit Gino in the chest who then struck out on purpose just to get out of there.

Paul, of the twins, froze as he watched the arc of the ball coming right at him. At the last moment, he twisted around and took it in the middle of his back, the thump echoing inside the hollow of his thin ribs. On the next pitch, Paul dropped the bat, fell to the ground and buried his head in his arms. The ball bounced off his helmet.

The parents, understandably, began voicing some concerns. I wasn't throwing that fast but granted, these were their kids I was hitting with a hardball. It had to look worse than it was.

"Quit hitting the kids, ya crazy shit-head bastard," someone yelled. A number of parents yelled back, "Hey! Language! Language!"

I wanted to yell, "It looks worse than it is, believe me," but that would just open up a debate. I had to ignore them and concentrate.

The umpire came out to the mound. "Having some trouble? Want a break, let someone else try for a while?"

I had never seen a coach take himself out of a game and there was nobody else. This was a fluke. It would pass. "I'll be all right."

"Out doing the town last night?" he said.

"Yeah, something like that," I lied.

I was past the point of thinking about it too much. I knew I was throwing too softly; if I used more speed, I'd be more accurate. They could handle it. I had to stop thinking about the plate. I had to stop thinking about the ball. I had to stop thinking about everything I could stop thinking about.

Next up was Clifford Blake with his sad, angelic eyes saying, "I know I'll get hit but please don't make it hurt too much." The suffering on the boy's face would have been inspiration to any religious painter in search of the ideal Saint Sebastian. But for me on that day, it provoked anger.

"Lose the attitude, Clifford. Quit looking at me that way. Suck it up," I yelled at him.

Then I wound up.

The cries from the stands as the ball left my hand said two things: first, it was faster than anything I'd thrown that day, which I knew; and second, they were expecting the worst. The pitch sailed past George's mitt and wedged in the link fence backstop while Clifford was already safely in the fetal position halfway back to the dugout. How he got there that fast still baffles me.

As the game progressed, I regained control and they started knocking them out of the infield. The score was tied eight to eight in the fifth inning and remained so until the bottom of the thirteenth. With Sean jigging away on first, Geno tagged one over the right field fence. And the game was finished. It was half past three.

Keeping their promise, Jeff and Mort cornered me and we had a talk adding to the growing evidence that baseball is, in many ways, like hunting.

When I got home that day, there was a notice from the county announcing they were going to pave the stretch of dirt road which meant the work-out birds, most likely, will be relocating.

I'll miss them.

I'll miss them along with the exhausting anticipation of one day running into Victoria again, knowing that if I obsess about it, it won't happen.

But until then, if ever, I have enough material to improvise upon: the woman who wanted to meet the man, deep in the woods by the lake on a summer's afternoon, with the promise that something surprising might happen. It was in her voice; it was in her eyes. He could actually feel it. It was already physically upon him. And there would be a good amount of dappled sunlight.

"Hilarious, humorous – this book has it all, and everything."

– *The Daily Beast*

"Two of the top humorists in America have created a stress-free way to enjoy stress."

– *Reader's Digest*

The Elements of Stress is a perfect respite from whichever unrelenting soul-crushing torment you're currently experiencing."

– *McSweeney's Internet Tendency,* editor Chris Monks

"Not to stress you out, but BUY THIS BOOK! IT'S VERY FUNNY!! BUY IT NOW!!!!"

– Jack Handey, author of *Deep Thoughts*

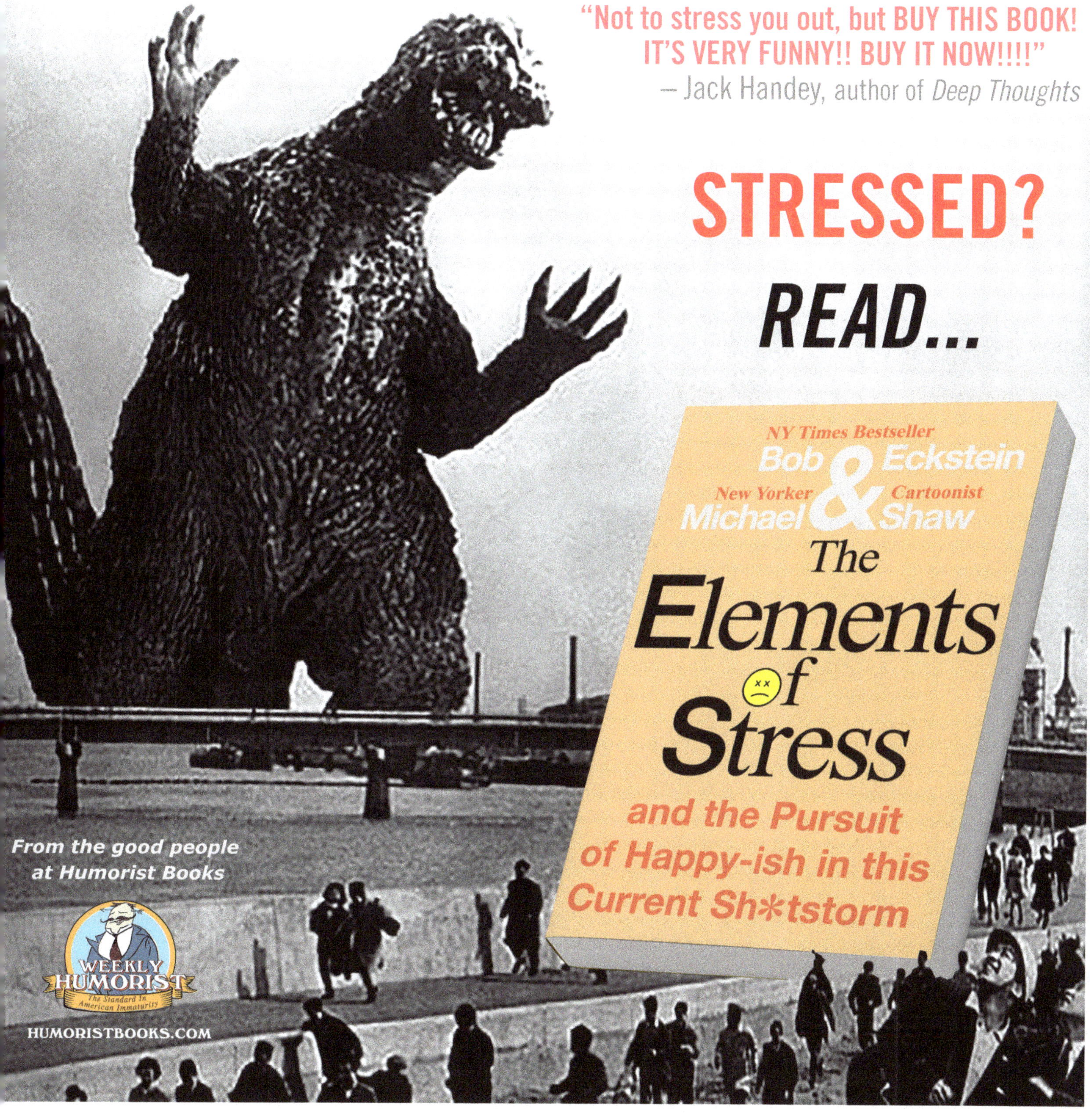
STRESSED?
READ...
NY Times Bestseller
Bob & Eckstein
New Yorker Cartoonist
Michael & Shaw
The Elements of Stress
and the Pursuit of Happy-ish in this Current Sh*tstorm
From the good people at Humorist Books
WEEKLY HUMORIST
HUMORISTBOOKS.COM

BRIAN McCONNACHIE

Cowboys on a Walnut Farm

Ripping through the still of daybreak, Urijah Van Zent rode in at a gallop, reined in his horse and hit the ground running. He'd thought about it enough. He wasn't going to think anymore. He aimed his heel at the bunkhouse door and kicked. It swung open, violently, hit the wall and bounced back tighter shut than before.

Some of the men sat up with a start but seeing nothing had changed, gratefully collapsed back to sleep. Except Blue-sky, who had not been asleep and for a moment saw Urijah's silhouette in the doorway and there appeared to be a gun in his hand. Blue-sky swung his feet from the bed and put on his boots.

"I didn't think he'd get it so soon," Blue-sky muttered. He thought he had another week before Urijah would return armed and with murderous intent. Blue-sky believed he had time to patch up the trouble between them. And if that didn't happen, he'd use the time to be long gone. But procrastination had always been his weakness as it was for many of the men who worked here. Where had the time gone? It was August already! Blue-sky had come to this Walnut Farm with the intention of staying a few months and saving a little money. But before he knew it, two years had slipped away. But that'll happen when you stay in one place too long. Familiarity can turn with a vengeance. Around the bunkhouse it was referred to as, "The Frustration of Misplaced Anger."

The cowboys who worked on this walnut farm had plenty of spare time. Probably too much time to overthink things. Minor things that easily inflate into brooding, important things if they weren't kept in check; if they weren't visited regularly with common sense and some humor.

The walnut cowboys considered themselves a special breed and spent a fair amount of time talking about it. They talked about who they were and why they did what they did. They talked about the pioneers who came before them and the methods they employed. They talked about the fortunes men have made speculating in walnut futures. It was a rare calling few men would confidently choose. But it was also a new era and the walnut was again, king.

Some of the men said they did it because they liked working out of doors and up in trees and bragged they could get so comfortable up there, they could even fall asleep. Others claimed it was the walnuts themselves that delighted and drew them here. How simple and intricate they were and how no two walnuts were ever alike—though the jury was still out on that popular notion. Still others found it far preferable to the more hazardous labors that might involve cattle drives, serving in the military, mining tunnels, law enforcement, open furnaces, knives, guns and hatchets. Gathering walnuts was reasonably safe and steady work. But to a man, they all liked the bunk time that went with it. Awake by 9, most of them didn't roll out of the sack till around 10:30. It also gave them lots of time to read. The walnuts weren't going anywhere. And those who did get an early jump on the job, were usually beat by early afternoon and spent the rest of their day asleep in trees or back in their bunks reading or napping a chunk of the day away or talking to one another about the pleasures and mysteries of this life, as well as the motives they had for choosing this work.

Some of the men worked in pairs; one upon the other's shoulders. Sometimes even in threes; the man, or men, above picking the walnuts and the man below, the strength, holding forth the bushel baskets catching the walnuts. Some, like Blue-sky, preferred to go solo. With a sack on his back, he'd climb a walnut tree and shimmy out on a limb. Still others, the ones with excellent balance, the ones who owned horses and guns, would stand atop the horse's saddle and tap, tap, tap the walnuts loose with the butts of their empty pistols. And for those fearful of heights, there were usually enough walnuts on the ground to satisfy their quota if they knew where to look (which wasn't always that obvious). One thing they all hoped to do was spot a sacred walnut. A walnut that might miraculously contain a miniature depiction from the Bible: Lot's wife being turned into salt; or Moses delivering the plagues upon Egypt; or Jesus carving a wooden box in which to store fish. These walnuts could fetch a lordly sum if they were in good condition and the image was arguably clear.

The door flew open again, and Urijah caught it as it came back at him. This time more of the men awoke, and they knew Urijah had gotten the money he needed to purchase a bullet and now would be the reckoning. They sat up in their bunks, fluffed their pillows and got comfortable.

Yes, Blue-sky realized, Urijah had a gun in his hand and as importantly, the bullet to go in it.

The nearest town that sold weapons and reliable ammunition was Tilman, some fifty-five miles away. There, the cost of a bullet—the round, the casing and the powder—came to about $48. Guns, they practically gave away. For the cowboys who worked on a walnut farm, this was a substantial sum to acquire; the decision to shoot someone with a bullet that expensive was a commitment not entered into lightly. The last shooting occurred more than four years ago, and no one now present was witness to what actually happened. One of the versions, however, was they each

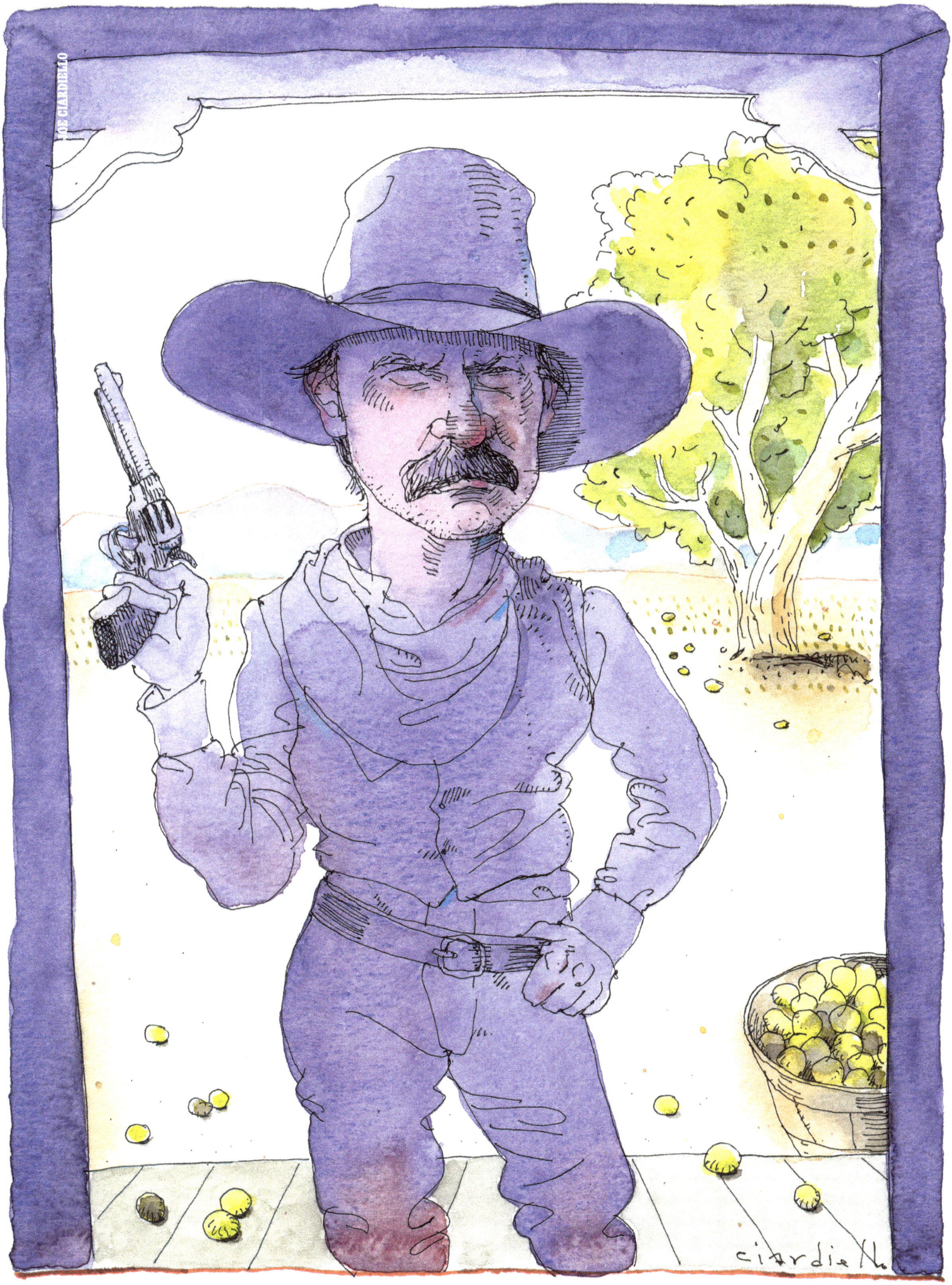
JOE CIARDIELLO
ciardiello

"You better not let Dad see you wearing that."

shot the other in their walnut-gathering hand, rendering each other unfit for this profession they were so suited to and loved. Both separately departed for other labors, leaving behind their cautionary tale.

More recently, there was a fight, but not with guns. The participants agreed it would be restricted to kicking, biting, nose- and ear-twisting, and punching. It also included, for a while, whacking each other over the head with smallish, tightly packed, burlap gift bags of fresh walnuts which the Troys, the owners, were test-marketing at the time and were being stored everywhere in abundance. The noise it made sounded far worse than the slight damage it inflicted. These two men, both considered to be "talkers," detested each other and disagreed on most everything. Their original conflict was, "Who actually said 'an unexamined life is not worth living,' Socrates or Plato?" Then the premise, "the unexamined life," became separated and wandered off, only to later reappear as a conundrum-provoking, "How unexamined can a life actually become?" The battle didn't include as much ear- and face-biting as some of the cowboys would have wished, but neither participant wanted their mouths to be occupied when they could be logically advancing the arguments each so tenaciously championed. In spite of the enthusiastic pounding the combatants gave and took, the battle raged for almost an hour. It was finally abandoned when both men, beaten into exhaustion, had to be carried to their bunks, where they were confined for several days and where each spent a fair part of that time, cursing the other and, in spite of the pain of bruised ribs, feebly tossed books at each other's heads.

Most of the men assumed that this fight, about to unfold before them, was over the affections of Dolores Troy, the daughter of Big Jake Troy, the owner of the eight-hundred-acre Oh So-Lazy-Oh Walnut Farm & Ranch-Oh.

Dolores Troy and her father lived in a fourteen-room, yellow Victorian farmhouse that was constructed with the promise that one day it would be filled with Big Jake's grandchildren. It sat centered in the circular shade of five oaks and one walnut tree, and stood about a quarter of a mile from the bunkhouse and mess hall. Dolores was a serious, efficient and oddly handsome woman in her mid-30s who rarely smiled but possessed a kind nature. She tended to the farm's business. She was tall but well coordinated, and could navigate a walnut tree as well as any man or maybe any primate. She weighed the walnuts, paid the men every Thursday evening (as they in turn tried to see down her blouse). She also kept from her father all offers—each more generous than the last—from manufacturers, worldwide, who wanted to haul off a large percentage of the walnut trees and make pianos out of them. Dolores's deceased mother, though declaring to enjoy music, in fact detested every piece of music she had ever heard, and made Dolores swear on a Bible she would never do anything that would remotely benefit the music industry.

It was also Dolores who interviewed new men for the job. She sometimes conducted these interviews on the upper limbs of the oak trees. Both Blue-sky and Urijah showed confidence ascending the trees and returning safely to the ground, which spoke well for them both.

"Why did you leave your last job?" she asked.

Blue-sky said he'd been a bugler in the United States Cavalry. Speaking on behalf of the other buglers, he complained to his commanding officer that, in addition to chipped teeth and split lips from the ever-elusive mouthpiece, the buglers found it nearly impossible to produce a sequence of notes on such a small musical instrument while bouncing about all herky-jerky on the back of a galloping horse over rugged terrain and be expected to play anything remotely recognizable as "Charge!" or "Retreat!" or "Go Left, Everybody."

"I don't know anything about any small musical instruments," Dolores suddenly interrupted, almost ending the interview—but when she was assured that he no longer played the bugle (especially on horseback or any other conveyance) she gave him the job. Then asked him to hurry down and send up the next candidate, Urijah.

Urijah told her this would be his first job. He was right out of college. He didn't speak much and had small interest in music.

Urijah, who slept up top, and Blue-sky below, had been bunkmates for as long as both had been there. They arrived at the ranch on the same day. Lying around as much as the walnut cowboys did, a few became skilled storytellers and speakers, while others developed as listeners and thoughtful, inquisitive, editors. For the most part it sorted itself out that the talkers bunked with the listeners.

Urijah grew into a talker, and Blue-sky initially appeared to be a most enlightened listener.

But when Urijah arrived he was far from being a talker; he was painfully shy and kept to himself. He was also distrusting. He ate alone. He avoided eye contact. He moved quickly past people, as if he expected they would slap the back of his neck to hurry him along; to hurry him out of their sight. If someone nearby suddenly raised a hand in gesture, Urijah was prone to flinch. At night, on occasion, he would scream in his sleep—but in this behavior, he was not alone. There were nights in the bunkhouse when the place sounded like a crazed zoo with half the men having nightmares, usually involving falling. On other nights could be added men leaping from their bunks trying to escape the sudden pain of leg cramps, and then colliding into one another as they hopped around in the dark.

Several of the men came to believe that Urijah Van Zent was shouldering a dramatic weight as he looked around for the right, deep enough hole to drop it into. Or person to leave it with. But until that happened, if ever, he'd not be fit company. He was judged as having too many demons to be working in such a tranquil place as a walnut farm.

"What is your name and where are you from?" Blue-sky asked him.

Urijah's response was barely audible. Aware of the man's shyness, Blue-sky didn't inquire further. He would, however, nod when he'd catch Urijah's eye. Gradually Urijah grew relaxed in Blue-sky's presence; he found Blue-sky comforting.

Some months later, the fellow in the next bottom bunk, Tyrel—a fellow Urijah suspected of having neck-slapping potential—got out of his bed and sat on the floor next to Blue-sky's bunk.

"May I speak with you?" said Tyrel.

Blue-sky nodded. "Yes. You may."

"I was lying in my bunk the other morning and thinking about the natural order of things. I realized we all have enemies. When we meet them we usually know it right off. And we can do little about it. Like that fight over Plato and Socrates a while ago. They were just fighting, it didn't matter about what. That was no, "Frustration of Misplaced Anger"—those two hate each other. Have you thought about this? Is there some eternal element, something I'm not considering while trying to understand why we naturally have enemies? Who are they and where do they come from?" Tyrel asked Blue-sky. "Why do we have enemies, and could the answer to this, in part, explain war?"

Blue-sky was silent with his thoughts.

"I will think about this," he said.

"Thank you. I appreciate it," said Tyrel.

From his bunk, Urijah listened and agreed with the man's quandary, but was also without resolution. But he was impressed that his bunkmate was held in such high regard as to be entrusted with a question of this magnitude.

Several days passed, and Urijah was lying on his bunk, reading and dozing, when Blue-sky returned from his day's labors. He'd been sleeping in trees the last two nights. He went to Tyrel's bunk. Tyrel was asleep, and Blue-sky shook his foot. The man awoke. Blue-sky stretched out on his own bed before speaking.

"Maybe our enemies are family members from past lives," Blue-sky said.

Urijah, hearing this, slapped a hand over his mouth and uttered, "Oh my God!" into it.

Propelled, Urijah jumped down and knelt by the side of Blue-sky's bunk. Knelt by the side of this wise man's bed and spoke urgently after months of silence.

"*Yes!* That's exactly who they are! It makes perfect sense. That's it, right there," Urijah began. "I have family in St. Louis. A big family. I left home. I was the only one who left. They're all still there. I don't know why they stay together. They all hate each other. This isn't past lives. This is going on right now," said Urijah. "But, yes! That's where our enemies come from. I see that clearly. Our own families are the seeds of it. Who knows us better and can do us more harm? How did you come to know this?"

Blue-sky shrugged. But from then on, Urijah Van Zent began to find his voice as well as the person he felt compelled to share it with.

He randomly began with stories of his family's behavior. He had never before done this. It had been drilled into him that behavior inside the family was no one else's business. It was a large family. There was a lot to keep quiet about. Urijah felt the importance of breaking the silence. Of bringing forth a number of experiences to share with Blue-sky. He started with the time his mother forced his youngest sister, then age 5, to eat an entire Vidalia onion because the child failed to tell her Mommy how much she loved her. Then there was an aunt, on his father's side, who had a

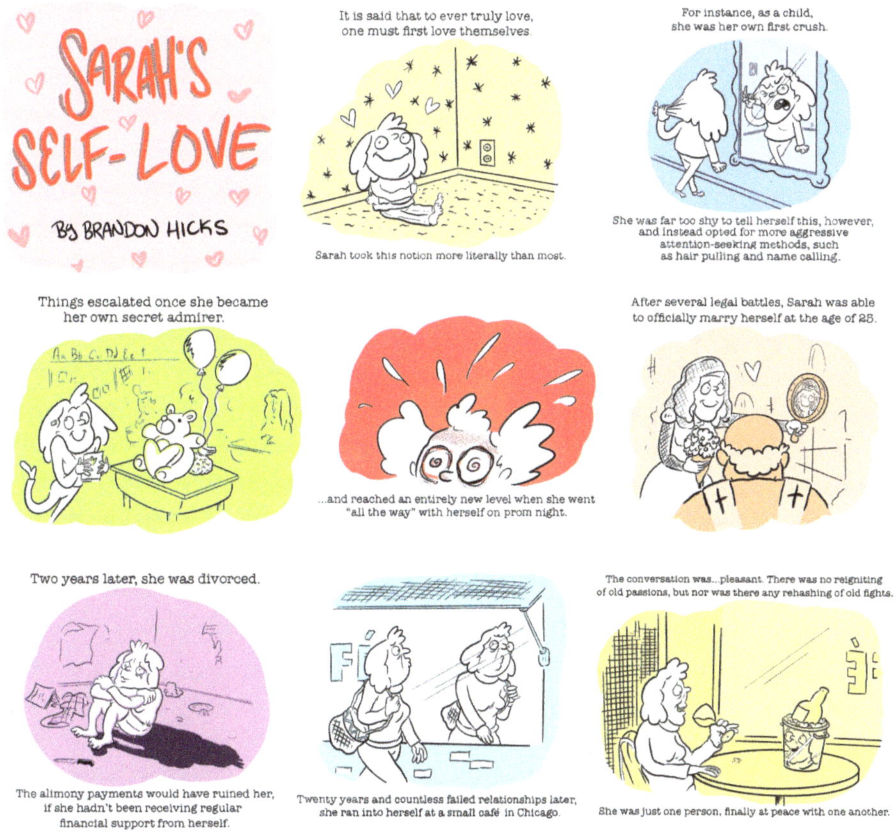
SARAH'S SELF-LOVE
BY BRANDON HICKS
It is said that to ever truly love, one must first love themselves.
Sarah took this notion more literally than most.
For instance, as a child, she was her own first crush.
She was far too shy to tell herself this, however, and instead opted for more aggressive attention-seeking methods, such as hair pulling and name calling.
Things escalated once she became her own secret admirer.
...and reached an entirely new level when she went "all the way" with herself on prom night.
After several legal battles, Sarah was able to officially marry herself at the age of 25.
Two years later, she was divorced.
The alimony payments would have ruined her, if she hadn't been receiving regular financial support from herself.
Twenty years and countless failed relationships later, she ran into herself at a small café in Chicago.
The conversation was...pleasant. There was no reigniting of old passions, but nor was there any rehashing of old fights.
She was just one person, finally at peace with one another.

penchant for wandering the house, late at night, slapping other relatives across the face while they slept—to pay them back for a slight, real or imagined, that may have occurred earlier that day or even years before or never.

Urijah's family confessions were usually done in the morning, before the day's walnut gathering began. He would sit on the floor at the side of Blue-sky's bed, and speak in a volume only Blue-sky was meant to hear. Each session, before he spoke, Uriah's instinct directed him to respectfully ask, "May I speak with you?"

Blue-sky would traditionally reply, "Yes, speak with me."

Over the next weeks and months, Blue-sky heard stories of cruelty, revenge and neglect, all emanating from the twisted core of the Van Zent household. The volume of this family's contemptible behavior was beginning to appear endless. But with Blue-sky now seeming to share this burden, the dramatic weight began lifting from Urijah. Urijah's nature was becoming renewed, showing self-confidence and friendliness. He nodded to his co-workers. Occasionally, and with some delicately, he patted their backs and wished them well on their day's gatherings. Some of the men found this awkwardness annoying, but it was an improvement over the sullen Urijah—and most of the cowboys found it hopeful to witness that such change is possible.

For a while, when Urijah collected his pay, he made sure he was last in line so he could have some time to speak with Dolores Troy (as well as look down her blouse). He greeted her with his biggest smile. He would ask her about the business. No one had shown this interest before, at least not to her, and she had plenty to report on the subject. She told him they were developing a hybrid walnut shell. It was more weather resistant and yet, easier to open. The plan was, she told him confidentially, to bring it to market next spring. It should be ready by then.

"Dad believes we'll be the chief beneficiary of this—but he also thinks it will be good for the entire industry," she said. "It'll get more people saying, 'Have you heard what's been going on with new King Walnut?' And isn't that what we all want to know? Will King Walnut be getting into the same special bag as cashews and pistachios, yea or nay?"

Then one morning, on a notable occasion, Urijah did not ask, "May I speak with you?" If he had, Blue-sky most probably would have replied, "No! No more," and put an end to this.

But neither happened, and Blue-sky's politeness was again subjected to the latest oppressive installment of the Van Zent chronicles.

"Now I'm going to tell you something really terrible. Are you ready for this?" Urijah began, "The holidays we all spent together..."

On more than a few occasions, cowboys pulled Blue-sky aside or climbed an adjacent tree and asked him, "What does Urijah say to you every morning?"

"I can't listen anymore," Blue-sky said. "I don't hear him after two sentences. But he never stops. Whatever he's saying, it's always awful, one bad thing after the next. The tone of his voice tells me how to react, and I make appropriate sounds in response," said Blue-sky.

"Be careful of him." Blue-sky was warned more than once. "Urijah's not really a walnut man. When a listener ignores a talker...well, you know what they say..."

"I'll be fine," Blue-sky would reply.

Late one Thursday evening, Blue-sky and Tyrel were discussing the changing value of industriousness over bravery in a world trying to become more civilized, (or was it?) when Urijah entered the bunkhouse talking out loud to himself. He sat on Blue-sky's bunk and continued speaking.

"...do you know where I've been? Do you know why I'm so late? I thought she'd never shut up. Yap yap yap about the walnuts. The walnuts this and the walnuts that. And then, who knows, maybe she'll build a house out of walnuts. Make shoes out of walnuts. Sure, why not? Then I have to swear to God I won't tell anybody, especially the men who work on the adjacent walnut farms, what we've got going on here. Otherwise, we might be looking at an out-and-out range war. 'And nobody wants that.' And, oh! By the way, we're all going to have to start signing, 'non-disclosure agreements.' Whatever those are."

As he spoke, Urijah saw Blue-sky's eyes shut—and he began nodding and humming in much the same fashion as when hearing the Van Zent calamities. Could it be possible Blue-sky wasn't listening, thought Urijah? Or could it be he just wasn't listening to this latest barrage of walnut claptrap?

To test him, Urijah asked in a mirthful tone, "Blue-sky, do you remember when I told you about that Christmas Father gave Mother a silk-lined box with a snake in it?"

Blue-sky responded with a warm reminiscent hum.

"And do you remember the time my one normal uncle who everyone thought was a lunatic took me on a wonderful holiday to Chicago?" he asked in a voice trying to be dense with pain.

Blue-sky sighed a condolence.

Urijah went to bed that night believing it wasn't possible that Blue-sky hadn't been listening; hadn't been sharing this huge burden. But that night, sleep would not come to Urijah. It wasn't till after daylight that he finally dozed off.

When Urijah awoke, later that morning, the bunkhouse was empty. His breathing was doglike, quick and shallow; he was having an experience he had not before known. He lay still as this reality gripped him deeper and squeezed him tighter. He understood—but didn't know how he understood—that from then on, he alone was responsible for all the internal functions of his own body. All those parts he knew or didn't know or had once heard mentioned: carotid artery, optic nerves, bone marrow, the liver and pancreas. Whatever, or whoever had effectively been in charge of running everything in sequence, or in unison or in balance was no longer present on the job. This once-automatic arrangement had unexplainably ended. A thought told him he had been alive long enough to now know how it all worked and to keep it working. And if he didn't, it was no one's fault but his own; he should have payed better attention. So he was now alone to manage his thalamus and kidneys and immune system and lungs and bone marrow and those many extra yards of different-size intestines. The whole caboodle. All he knew was, the brain sent out signals and the rest obeyed. But he had nothing to tell his brain that would achieve this. "Digest the meal I ate and keep my heart beating," was not going to be specific enough for this new arrangement. But if it were possible to give the correct directions, would his brain even obey? Could the soul maybe jump in here and on occasion outrank the brain, and get things back on track? It would show some real character. But there was great risk in this. There was a lot that could go wrong. There is probably an entire chapter on keeping the appendix from suddenly rupturing and even more on not mixing up the blood flow with the body's waste. The simple truth remained, Urijah knew nothing. But if he didn't learn something soon, these would be the final moments of his short, tortured, misspent life. He'd stop breathing. For a moment he paused in his terror to curse his family for not sending him to medical school, then returned to his dilemma. Maybe he could find an ally like the pituitary gland, whatever that was. Or enlist enzymes, whatever they were, and get them on his side. In turn, maybe they could get their working colleagues to come over to his side. But this was risky, considering he'd be starting from nothing.

The grip on his chest tightened. He crossed his arms upon his chest in a fatal pose and shut his eyes, waiting for the inevitable as he grew helpless and angrier at this happening to him.

Urijah Van Zent took the bullet from his pocket, waved it teasingly, then put it in the chamber. Blue-sky moved to the side and began climbing over bunks heading towards the back wall. Urijah followed.

"Get away!" "Out in the middle!" "Fight over there!" "Don't you come near here with that gun!" ordered the men who were being climbed over.

"You'll be picking walnuts this day in Hell with the Devil," said Urijah to Blue-sky, ignoring the cowboys' yells.

"They pick *coal*, not walnuts, ya dope," a voice corrected.

"That's why it's Hell," another voice offered.

"Did you listen to *any* of it?"

"Yes!" said Blue-sky, continuing to back away.

"Then," demanded Urijah, "what happened to my grandmother during Christmas dinner that time?"

"She choked on a bone!"

"No!"

"No one would listen to her!"

"NO!"

"She dropped dead and no one stopped eating!"

"Actually, that's pretty close..." said Urijah. "But you're guessing."

"I'm warning you, Urijah, don't shoot."

Windowless and doorless, the back wall put an end to Blue-sky's retreat. He brought up his arms to protect his head, then slid down the wall drawing his knees tight to him, trying to become as small an object as possible.

"Hey Blue-sky!" someone yelled. "Can you see into the abyss? What's it like?"

Urijah took careful aim.

Everyone flinched at the report of the gun.

If Blue-sky had been posing for a life-size depiction of Christ's crucifixion, and Urijah had been allowed to bring the gun as close as three feet, he still would have missed by an embarrassing margin.

Blue-sky slowly unfolded himself. He got to his hands and knees and crawled back to his bunk.

Urijah looked at the gun in disbelief: How did *that* happen? He held it by the trigger guard away from him as if it were contaminated.

The men started jeering and laughing and kicking their blankets in the air.

With unconvincing jollity, Urijah asked: "Bet you thought you were a goner, huh? Ha, ha! I had you going, didn't I? Oh, did I tell you what Dolores said about the new walnut hybrid? It's actually kind of interesting..."

Blue-sky emptied the money from his secret pouch and started counting it on the bed.

"What do you think, Blue-sky, how long?" asked Tyrel from his bunk.

"Two weeks! Maybe a week and a half if I put in extra walnut time," said Blue-sky.

"Is that counting the time to Tilman and back?"

Urijah didn't know if he should run for it or keep changing the subject until he hit on something truly engaging. B

"Howdy there, Ms. O'Keeffe! Boy, those vaginas are sure comin' in nice this year!"

Life of Brian

Mary sent out the email: "They're doing an issue for my Dad—any anecdotes or greetings you'd like to share? Naturally, this is TOP SECRET."

JACK HANDEY

It's important that we remember that the legendary Brian McConnachie is just that: a legend. He's imaginary, not a real person. A fanciful invention of our times.

It's soothing to think that there really is a Brian McConnachie, tall and amiable, living deep in the forest, typing out hilarious stories. But that's a myth.

"But wait, I know Brian, I've worked with him," someone might say. Or "He's my husband" or "He's my father." It's amazing the lengths people will go to preserve their beliefs.

Some people say that I claim Brian is imaginary because I owe him a lot of money, and that I have plagiarized several of his stories. If only it were that simple.

One day, perhaps, a real Brian McConnachie will come and dwell amongst us. But until then, we have the legend.

LAWRENCE MURPHY

(Larry met Brian at the LaSalle Military Academy in 1957. They remain friends to this day.)

Each day, Brian and I marched together in uniform across a vast expanse of green grass, LaSalle's parade grounds on the south shore of Long Island. He particularly enjoyed the works of John Philips Sousa; I know this because fifty years later, Brian can still hum most of the tunes!

If the weather was hot, the military authorities too strict in their daily inspection, or dragging out the interminable waiting at "attention" rather than the more relaxed "parade rest," one of us would attempt to organize the classic way out: One of the tinier cadet privates in the platoon would be asked to lock his knees tightly. His circulation would be cut off, causing him to shortly thereafter topple unconscious onto the soft turf below. The private would then be carried off to the infirmary by at least two bigger cadets pre-selected for the detail, thus relieving these cadets from the ordeal.

Brian's masterstroke was simple: Why not have *a big guy* take the plunge? Passed out, he'd need at least one cadet on each extremity to haul him away. Instead of one or two, five or maybe six happy cadets would find themselves suddenly "off duty without penalty."

In the infimary, Brian awakened humming "Stars & Stripes Forever" with a very contented, placid smile covering his visage .When he hears this Sousa tune today, that contented look still returns—and I know exactly why.

ROB MARIANI

Brian and I met at our first out-of-college jobs: copyboys at *The New York Daily Mirror*. The work was beyond boring and we partied a lot after work. While Brian lived on the Upper West Side, I was living across Central Park—East 89th Street, to be exact, on the fifth floor of a six-story building.

One night, we decided to throw a "roof party." It was a masterstroke; all we had to do was lug our booze and snacks up one more flight, and the tar-papered roof became our rowdy "penthouse."

As we all got drunker and dizzier, Brian suddenly leapt up about three feet, onto the edge of the roof's concrete barrier, which was maybe six inches wide! Martini in hand, he walked—actually he staggered—across the narrow roof line with nothing between him and a plunge to certain death!

He hobbled down, laughing. I looked up at his face and said, "Brian, I will *never* forgive you for that."

Just a few months ago, I was talking with Brian on the phone and with no particular context reminded him once again of my promise never to forgive him. Once again, he laughed. And I didn't.

MIKE BRACY

I've been a close friend of Brian's for more than 50 years, and so have countless funny memories of my times with Brian. A lot of them are subtle—Brian is not a loud man—so they don't lend themselves to retelling. But I'll try.

One night in the late '60s, we were having dinner (actually mostly drinks) at the McConnachie's apartment in the West 50s, when, for some reason, Brian decided to challenge me to a race around the block. When we got to the street, he suggested that we run in opposite directions. I naively ran off at full speed around the block. When I got back to the door, Brian was, of course, already there and claimed victory. Only later did I remember that I hadn't seen Brian on the other side of the block.

That's the last time I raced Brian.

JACK ZIEGLER

(The late cartoonist Jack Ziegler was one of Brian's closest friends; these extracts are from Jack's autobiography.)

So Brian and I, on our separate coasts, were fairly unhappy, toiling at jobs that needed to be disappeared so that

[Thanks to Maxx, Jessica and all Zieglers for letting us print the excerpts from Jack's book. I couldn't fit this on page 4!—Ed.]

Brian McConnachie
at home in Florida, May 2020.
Photo by B.A. VAN SISE.

we could get on with the true purpose of our lives, which was to write and have the freedom to do so.

Ever since my wife and I left the East Coast for San Francisco in early '69, Brian and I had kept a steady correspondence chronicling our so-far unfulfilled hopes, letters heavily weighted with dire, woebegone complaints. We soon hit on the idea of using any subsequent communiques as a playground of sorts, a field on which to let our imaginations run free and write whatever the hell we pleased, wet our whistles on the craft, hone whatever dormant skills might be lurking, and maybe at the same time hit on some possible springboards for ideas. Or, at the very least, a snappy turn of phrase here and there.

We got off to an enthusiastic, if a bit murky and wordy, beginning, but soon a few things appeared in our mailboxes that started to make sense. The following letter from Brian, for instance, gives a hint of the flavor of some of the quirky greatness that would subsequently emerge. This letter arrived in January 1970, and is a consideration of a recently shuttered piano bar we occasionally patronized in college. (My most vivid memory from that place is the night I lost my temper when a rogue cigarette machine stole my quarters. Like some sort of crazed delinquent, I decided to teach it a lesson by kicking its face in. But that's an unpleasant tale that presents me in a harsh, unflattering light and, therefore, hardly worth repeating.)

"Do you remember," Brian wrote, "when we were fast-dealing, high-struttin', finger-snappin', wise-crackin', trouble-duckin', double-dealin', kiss-stealin', smart-ass, cock-o-the-walk, no-cheese-face kids? Do ya? And we'd come sailing into that Forest Hills Inn like two supersonic Jumbo 747 Pan Am convoy carriers. Plop our tail feathers down in that subterranean joy den and proceed to win the 'Name That Song or Show or Movie or Whatever' contest. And we'd cheat, lie, copy, curse, spit in the other players' faces, wet ourselves, throw things, throw up, reach inside the piano for clues, crawl along the floor, howl, growl, bite legs, etc., etc.

"But we won. The Champagne Twins. Laughing, reeling, pitching, and puking our innards up, our venerable guts forming new art patterns on the sidewalks of Forest Hills.

"The other players would moan when we'd enter the arena. 'We don't have a chance against the Champagne Twins. You don't know what it's like to play them. If you're smart, you won't.'

"Those were the days, my friend, with everybody snapping, 'Yezzir, yezzir, Massah Jack. Massah Jack need a new pencil?'

"You'd let fly with a kick to the groin, screaming into his contorted face, 'Yes, Mr. Toad, I do', and yell to the other players, 'Game suspended 'til I get a new pencil.' And I'd dash around the piano to copy all of their answers, then tear up their sheets. Do you remember those crazy times?

"Well, forget them! They're over. So quit deluding yourself—living in some senseless daydream, forchristssake. THE WHOLE PLACE IS CLOSED DOWN, THE BAR, THE DINING ROOM, THE DOWNSTAIRS. BOARDED UP. FINISHED. IRON GATES ACROSS THE ENTRANCES. Cats wander about, brushing against empty bottles that spin in their wake.

"Ghost town. A giant drunk sleeping in the pee of the past. Sunset Boulevard, featuring the Gloria Swanson Room, the Ken Murray Bar, the Buster Keaton Grill. They all stayed open years too long. No transplants. It's dead.

"Your old friend Ryan is locked in. Sobbing softly, he has a novelty-shop rubber breast in each hand. He places the tits up against his chest and looks down through his tears, but isn't amused. Big drops roll down his wrinkled face. He puts them on his knees, the tips of his dusty shoes. On his hips he draws them like six-guns, arranging a new anatomy. He quietly cries and doesn't try to leave. He puts them over his ears and then his eyes and the insides catch his tears.

"Big pink eyes with red nipples—a giant space bug in contemporary baggy pants.

"Passing by, I'll stare in at him for a moment through the iron gate, but he'll look past me with his swollen eyes. No recognition. No 'Oh hi, yeah hi. You're Jackie's friend, huh?'

"Nothing. And I won't 'Hi, Mr. Ryan, whatcha doin' in there?' It's all over and he's just returned for entombment. Maybe they won't even go in for his body after he dies there. All the cats will just sit on him while he's warm and then cave him in, push the breasts around with their paws, then lose interest and wander off. Maybe the trees around the Inn will bloom in the spring.

"Maybe they won't."

Almost a decade later, a version of this letter introduced my first collection of drawings, *Hamburger Madness*.

Some six months later another letter arrived with the news that Brian and Benton & Bowles had parted ways. This left him kind of flatlined, neither happy nor unhappy; he was surprised to find himself curiously devoid of apprehension. He said the recent visit with us in San Francisco had seminally changed his attitude and once he got back to New York his days at work started to fill him with contempt. The people at B&B took notice rather quickly, and shortly

BILL WOODMAN

BRIAN AND I ONCE BARTENDED AT A GATHERING ON THE UPPER WESTSIDE — MANHATTAN.

thereafter he was let go.

During their stay with us, Brian, his wife Ann, my wife Jean Ann, and I went on a picnic one day to Baker Beach, with its magnificent views of the Golden Gate Bridge and the hills of Marin.

We had been drinking wine there for a couple of hours and smoking some grass, generally laughing our asses off and having the time of our lives, when a bearded, buckskinned young hippie in a cowboy hat, a total stranger, decided to take a seat on our blanket and join in on the carousing. This was not unusual in those days and we didn't mind because this guy had a good sense of humor and also a little extra weed that he was delighted to share. He eventually asked us where we were from and what we did and Brian pointed across the bay and told him that he worked in an office building that was "as tall as that hill over there" and that he did "gee, I guess nothing." Apparently that was a defining moment. The words seemed to have lifted a sort of veil from his eyes. The next day he and Ann went back to New York and he quickly got himself fired. That was when Brian started to write in earnest.

RICK MEYEROWITZ

If the story of the *Lampoon* were a script by Rod Serling, the main character would've been Brian McConnachie, a man who, his colleagues were convinced, was from another planet. Whether this is true or not, I can't say. Or won't say. Or am not allowed to say. I will only tell you that in a group saturated in brilliant chatter, only Brian could leave the others speechless.

He was a tall man, elegantly put together, firmly bow-tied, stately and somewhat diffident in manner. A patrician; he stood out in the cramped, characterless office space inhabited by what seemed to be a bunch of otherwise unemployable misfits. What Brian brought to the magazine was an outsider's point of view—some thought far outside—in fact, from a different dimension.

His dream-like and odd scenarios left some readers confused, but laughing. By emphasizing the illogical and the absurd, and demolishing everyone's cozy expectations, he became the salaried on-staff Dadaist of *The National*

MARY O'HARA

Dear Daddy:

Mary (left) and Brian, 1984.

One Christmas, you gave me a framed image of your favorite line from the play *Our Town* in your lovely cursive writing: "Oh world, you are too wonderful for anyone to realize you." This quote remains the centerpiece of a wall of family photos in my home. Everyone who knows you well would agree that you embody the wonder, the appreciation, and the small preciousness of life found in this quote.

Because of your sense of wonder, my childhood was filled with imagination, magical stories and unanswerable questions. It was filled with evening walks to look up at the moon, promises to sew homemade stuffed animals out of old socks that were even bigger than the ones at F.A.O. Schwarz, and a sturdy wooden swing you made that hung from my loft bed, just far away enough from a nearby fourth story window to be safe.

Your wonder took us to Paris, where I found my sixteen-year-old self mesmerized walking through the stacks at Shakespeare and Company. We left with a book on the philosopher Montaigne, just because we thought the name was so funny to say. On that same trip, you walked Alan Goldberg and I all over Paris to find a bistro that offered a half-price menu after 11:30 p.m. You charmed the owners by speaking English in a French accent and they served us a delicious dinner, probably too wonderful for anyone to realize.

Because of your sense of appreciation, I learned to cry on cue at every movie that you cry at, swoon at lyrics you pointed out to me, and pause at prose that you read to me, over and over. Once you forced me to memorize and perform a scene from *Our Town*, which I resisted—but I trusted you enough to see it through.

From your sense of life's preciousness, you willingly stayed up many a late night with me in high school, to help me edit my term papers. When it was time to begin college tours, you took me on a road trip through New England that we still laugh about today, but we can barely remember why. Your birthday gifts have been wonderful: at 16, collections of letters to me from my dearest friends; and at 21, a journal of my life told through your eyes. That remains the most incredible gift I have ever received.

Because of you, my deepest laugh is just as loud and booming and joyful as yours. Making you laugh is one of my favorite things and when we laugh together, it becomes an uncontrollable seesaw of mirth, too wonderful for either of us to stop.

Daddy, you are a brilliant and kind soul and a gift to us all. Both George Bailey and Thorton Wilder were right: It's a wonderful life…because you have helped us all realize how truly wonderful it can be.

Lampoon. Our Duchamp.

Brian told Tony Hendra that he'd come to the magazine from the "Floor of Lost Men" at Benton & Bowles, the ad agency he'd been laboring at. (What could he have been writing for them?) At the *Lampoon,* he and his work were so appealingly different from anything, or anyone, else that he quickly became every other writer's favorite writer. He'd found a home.

The surprising thing is that once he found it, he didn't stay forever. He was at the *Lampoon* only four years. He left to pursue television writing, acting, and to spend more time with his family. The work Brian did in those too few years is still vibrant, and incredibly funny. It may even be timeless. In any case, it's well loved, here on Earth, and on his home planet.

JACK ZIEGLER

I picked up *The Lampoon* because I knew that there'd be a Brian story in there, something to do with the recent death of opera singer Ezio Pinza, and maybe one of his cartoons. I thumbed through it at the kitchen table, the late afternoon sun streaming over the treetops from the park across the street and through our open window, lighting up the pages in my hands. I read the piece immediately, then reread it. It was, and remains to this day, one of the funniest things I've ever read. It was just a short, simple article concerning people's reactions to the terrible news of Pinza's death, something on the order of "Where Were You When JFK Got Shot?" I wrote and told him it seemed to me like a series of cartoons, but done in prose, a bunch of quick visits with these interviewees and what they had to say about this dreadful event. Snippets.

And that's basically what constitutes a cartoon. It's a snippet. In general, it depicts a single moment in the lives of the protagonists—the best cartoons providing enough of a thumbnail history so that the reader knows everything he needs to know about what went on before and what will probably transpire afterwards. This is all provided in the drawing by the demeanor, clothing, room furnishings, etc., and is so inherent in the whole concept of cartooning that the reader remains unaware of what is automatically intuited about these characters. And therein lies the satisfaction. This holds true for both the creator and his audience.

I took the "Pinza" piece to heart. The humor had a wild abandon and made me laugh out loud. I'd seen cartoons that could do the same thing for me, but very few. There were probably others out there somewhere, too, but where? France? China? The Angry Red Planet Mars? If they did exist, I wanted to find them. And if I couldn't find them, then maybe I'd try to do them myself.

From that "Pinza" moment on, I reversed myself and stopped considering what might appeal to others. If I was going to become the artist I envisioned, be it cartoonist, writer, whatever, the time had arrived to start taking care of Customer #1: me.

Legendary illustrator Frank Springer was one of Brian's frequent collaborators at the **Lampoon** *and after. This team-up was created for the 1982 pilot issue of* **The American Bystander.**

ELLA BRACY

Brian's wife Ann and I were in college together, then roomed in D.C. for a few years. When we began dating our future husbands, my Mike and her Brian, they two became close friends. A few years later we all moved to NYC, and lived maybe five blocks from each other.

We often had each other over for dinner and one time on a very cold night, we invited Brian and Ann over. We had a fireplace and, during cocktails, I noticed we were running out of wood. Brian jumped up and said he would be right back.

We of course thought he was going to the corner store, to buy a Duraflame. Instead, Brian came back a half hour later with a chest of drawers. "I saw it on the street, put out for the trash."

We all laughed hysterically, but it became clear that Brian was serious. I had to tell him that I didn't want to take hammer and saw on the thing, especially in our small apartment and on my mother's oriental rug. Nor did we want to burn the house down.

Brian, being Brian, was disheartened and a little hurt at our lack of adventure. The chest of drawers went out to the street the next day.

JACK ZIEGLER

I continued to forge on and every other week drove into the city to make the rounds of the magazines, peddling my latest suspect wares. My last stop was always *The National Lampoon*, on Madison Avenue, where I would hook up with Brian, show him my latest, then we'd go around the corner to the Coral Cafe on 58th St., which had become the *Lampoon* hangout. Most nights we'd be joined there by others on the editorial staff—Henry Beard, Doug Kenney, Michael O'Donoghue, Ann Beatts, Tony Hendra, Sean Kelly, and the art directors, Michael Gross and David Kaestle. Drinks would be flowing, with ideas for next month's issue tossed back and forth in blazing rapid-fire bursts. No notes were ever taken during these boozefests and rarely did any of these unbridled ideas see print in forthcoming issues. Raucous

DAVE THOMAS
Vikings and Beekeepers

Catherine O'Hara descends into the fog.

This is a story of how a wonderful idea for a sketch from the mind of a brilliant writer can emerge as one of the more hilarious and memorable scenes in the run of a show and, at the same time, one of its biggest production nightmares.

Brian joined *SCTV* in 1981 when the show was picked up for NBC's Friday late-night lineup. Pretty early into his run, Brian came to me with an idea for a sketch. "It's called 'Vikings and Beekeepers' and it goes something like this: In the Year 986, the Vikings, bored with their routine, and, wanting to torment the English even more, decided to add bees to their raids."

Bees? This was such a delightfully insane concept that I fell in love with it right away and offered to help Brian write it.

"Vikings and Beekeepers" became one of *SCTV*'s classic sketches…and perhaps the biggest production headache in the history of the show. First, a forty-foot Viking longboat had to be built (it still exists today and is used in parades in Edmonton). To complicate matters further, the production crew decided to put the ship on a giant gimbal to simulate the motion of the ocean. Bad idea. The gimbal made the ship so tall it banged into the grid, and the pedestal-mounted Ikegami video cameras were too low to shoot the crew in the ship.

Then there were the hellish details of the sketch. The beekeepers demanded that the bees could only travel east by night, so, in the day, the Vikings had to row backwards; disputes broke out between the Beekeepers and Vikings and those had to be carefully choreographed; Catherine O'Hara had to be flown in from the grid on a wire as Brunhilda, a Viking conflict mediator; and the studio needed to be filled with smoke to simulate fog and to hide the studio floor in the wide shots. Plus, the air conditioning was down—so the cast playing the Vikings began to get very hot in their helmets, glued-on beards and heavy fur costumes.

We were originally scheduled to wrap at 7 p.m., but that came and went. By midnight the producers decided that to stay on schedule, we had to finish the scene that night. Best estimates now predicted a 6 a.m. wrap.

John Candy, who was playing one of the Vikings, was the most uncomfortable in his costume, and characteristically subversive. He didn't want to spend the night shooting this scene, so he called the Four Seasons Hotel in Edmonton and hired the bartender (who was a friend of his) to come to the studio and set up a full bar. We all joined in John's act of rebellion against the producers' decision to go all night. The bar was up and running by 1:00 a.m.

By 3:00 a.m. everybody was pretty drunk, and there was at least another three hours of shooting to complete the scene. But it all came to an abrupt end when the hairdresser (who was doing double-duty as a Viking because he already had a beard) threw up in the longboat. The producers decided to call it a wrap.

Brian wasn't there for the shoot and missed seeing his wonderful idea degenerate into hilarious fatigue and rebelliousness. He would've loved that. We never shot the ending and later decided to end on the song "Vikings and Beekeepers." But we got enough of it on tape to preserve Brian's idea and, to this day, it's one of the sketches that the *SCTV* cast remembers and laughs about most. Thank you, Brian.

and rude-boy hilarity was the order of the day, much more so here at the Coral than what was actually appearing in the mag. Or so it seemed to me.

PHOEBE GEER

(Phoebe is a longtime friend of Brian's daughter Mary.)

Every kid should be lucky enough to have a friend with a dad like Brian McConnachie. He's the dad who did things your own father would never allow: He'd teach you and your 5th grade buddy, sitting on piles of phonebooks in the driver seat, how to steer an old Volvo around a shopping mall parking lot. He'd hollow out the center of a giant bush in his yard to create a fantastical topiary secret clubhouse, straight out of a Tim Burton movie. He'd hand you scissors to clip bikini-clad magazine pictures of Sophia Loren and actually let you glue them on his bathroom wall. He'd show you the grown-up comedies that taught you how good movies can be. He'd laugh at your jokes—authentic belly laughs that proved you were a cool and funny human—not just a smart kid. He'd sit with you and your friend at his kitchen table and ask you all sorts of questions about your opinions, thoughts and dreams. He'd really be interested in the answers. He'd teach you how to be a great parent. The kind a long-grown kid will never forget.

JACK ZIEGLER

After resigning from *Saturday Night Live*, Brian decided to set out on his own by starting up an oversized publication dedicated to art, humor, and witty comment. It was called *The American Bystander*, and began its short life as a big family affair with much of the initial monetary backing coming from current and former *SNL*ers. Jean Ann and I also threw in a little cash, a small thank-you for the mortgage down payment Brian and Ann had graciously lent us seven years before, as well as a supportive tip of the hat for this bold, new venture, which I had no doubt Brian could easily pull off. The staff was dotted with other friends and acquaintances, too, from Barbara Shelley as art director to her soon-to-be ex-hubby Bill as comics editor. The rest of the masthead looked like it was lifted directly out of Brian's home rolodex—writers, artists, performers, various chums, and a bunch of other ne'er-do-wells whose paths he'd crossed in the past few years while working in television or advertising or at the *Lampoon*.

John Belushi, one of Brian's earliest backers, was now making movies out in Hollywood and, a few weeks prior to publication, he OD'd and died at his apartment in the Chateau Marmont. A couple of weeks after that, Brian gave Barbara, his AD, the boot. But why, I wondered, would he do that? Was it a case of nerves? Pressure? Fear? I never found out, but then I never asked, either.

The pilot issue, designed to attract further financing, came out in the spring of 1982 and was a beautiful thing to behold, full of oddball articles and spreads and even odder-ball cartoons and full-color comics. I liked it, but as I look at it now, I recognize that it might have been just too strange an entity back then for most potential investors. And without their participation, *The Bystander* never made it to Issue #2.

Maybe the loss of Belushi and Barbara were portents of trouble ahead—who's to say? Given time, *The Bystander* might have evolved into something special; I'd like to think so. It had the

ROZ CHAST

Many decades ago, while day drinking in Tin Pan Alley with a group of cartoonists and other strays, Brian tried to convince me to fly over the Gowanus Canal for an article that would appear in *The American Bystander*. A number of helium-filled balloons would be tied around me in such a way that I would float up in the air and over the Gowanus Canal. I declined.

potential, but, omens aside and given the boom-or-bust crapshoot of the start-up, it was simply not to be.

JENNY BOYLAN

Brian McConnachie was the first person who ever took me to an opera. His wife Ann was out of town the night he had tickets to La Bohéme, and so it fell to me to serve as his fallback date for the evening.

In those days I was just scraping by on a single slice of pizza a day while I worked during the days at the 1981 version of *American Bystander* (where my hilarious title was "managing editor.") In the evenings I tried to write a novel about a wizard who owned an enchanted waffle iron. I was pretty raggedy.

Brian and I met at the fountain, and walked through the glorious lobby with its starburst chandelier. We settled into our velvet seats. The lights went down and the music began.

Many years later, the first time I went scuba diving, I had the experience of swimming out over an unexpected abyss on the ocean floor, and feeling the sensation of looking down into an almost unmeasurable chasm. That's what it was like to hear *La Bohéme* for the first time. And it was not lost on me that in the harrowing, noble-but-doomed dreams of the protagonists on stage, I was seeing a story of people not so unlike my 25-year-old self. It made me feel a little self-conscious, having such an emotional reaction to the music, but that's who I was then: a young person who had given up everything in order to become an artist, a writer living very close to poverty in the great city, all in hopes of creating something important and beautiful—and *The American Bystander* not least.

I held the tears back for a couple acts, but toward the end, as Mimi staggered through a snowstorm, alone, the dam burst. Did I already know that she wasn't going to survive Act IV? I looked on stage and saw myself—hungry, hopeful, and so in love. Did I see in the fate of Puccini's bohemians what lay in store for *The American Bystander* itself?

I don't know. All I know is that the tears rolled down and fell in my lap.

I looked over at Brian. He was crying, too.

JACK ZIEGLER

Brian, Bill Woodman, John Caldwell (another cartoonist pal), and I were having lunch after rounds one Wednesday at the River Cafe in Brooklyn. We were dawdling over our postprandial drinks with a lot of time on our hands when we decided to form a gang, calling ourselves the Glory Boys, a traveling band of nonchalant superhero crimefighters. If we ever noticed something bad going down, we were to toss aside our cartoon-carrying briefcases or shoulder bags and give chase to the evildoers, following them into no matter how dark-

............◆............

Kind, approachable, with a glint of the whimsical and fantastic, sort of like a flying boy.

............◆............

ened an alley they might run, shouting after them at the top of our lungs and in unison what was to be our slogan: "Gllllloooooooooooorrrrrrrrrrrryyyyy!!" Anyway, that was the intention fueled by our late afternoon cups, but the closest we ever came to any action was one day when we stopped dead in our tracks and thought about rescuing a cat we happened to notice perched high up in a tree. Our posse may have had no legs, but its name lives on, thanks to John, who later dedicated one of his books, a cartoon collection called "Mug Shots," to our short-lived gang. Gllllooorry!

ART SILVERMAN

(Art is a longtime producer for National Public Radio.)

Brian found the secret passage to my heart. Or at least my left ventricle. Here I was, a serious producer of serious NPR programs, when a voice on the phone proposes a story on the "running of the bulls in Grover's Corners." I understood the words, and that there was a human on the other end of the call. But nothing more made sense.

I was intrigued, and professionally suicidal. I accepted the pitch. On March 29, 2002, NPR listeners tuned in to hear something special. (*We've reprinted the sketch in full on page 16.—Ed.*)

It wasn't the first nor the last moment of perplexing and hard-to-fight-for unreality Brian would send my way. It was among the minority of pitches that actually made it to air. So many calls to me out of the blue—so few chances to convince my editors that what Brian was proposing would be logical for us to put on the radio. It was never a winning strategy to argue "logic" on these matters.

I am pleased I could get some of the ideas on the air. I regret that the "Real Story of the Three Stooges" never made it. (That's the one where it was revealed none of the stunts the boys did were fake, and it chronicled the medical records to prove it.) I also regret we never had a chance to have America hear how a young Brian fixed the World Series.

But seven wonderful times, I turned the power of NPR into a weapon of mass confusion.

No one like Brian has come my way since.

TIMOTHY O'HARA

My favorite memory of Brian McConnachie is from a moment that only he and I shared. It was when I asked for his only daughter's hand in marriage. It was 2007, around the Christmas holiday. I had traveled with Mary from Chicago to their family's home on Nelson Lane in Garrison, N.Y.

I decided that I was going to ask Brian the big question at night, after everyone else had gone to bed. I remember being nervous that day about how he would react—I had this secret in my head that was going be big news, at least in both of our worlds—and the timing and delivery of the request were key. There were plenty of moments when we were alone, but it just didn't feel right to ask him during a football game, even it was during a commercial.

So I held the secret until the nighttime, after Ann and Mary went to bed. I approached him by the sink as he made us a nightcap. I started talking. I knew my lips were moving, but I was focused on reading his reaction. I tried to convey how much I loved his daughter and that I wanted to spend my life with her. About how wonderful she was. As I spoke, he began to smile, which I thought was a good sign.

He said yes, he would give me his blessing to marry his only daughter. I will never forget how kind he was to me during that tense moment. We hugged right there next to the sink. There was a brief, but appropriate, discussion of the dowry, and then we had a drink. It is such a warm memory.

Mary and I were married that next October at a church that was only a short walk from Nelson Lane. We had the wedding reception at that same house. As we celebrated under a tent in the back yard, I looked back to the kitchen and saw the spot near the sink where we had that wonderful memory. I looked to find Brian and saw him doing the moonwalk on the dancefloor. I knew I had found my place.

SAM EVANS

I grew up down the block from the McConnachies. Mary and I were childhood friends and our parents were friends. We stayed friends after they left the city but have grown apart with time, life, etc.

Brian recently re-entered our household and met our kids (2 and 4) through Danny. Danny is a flying boy in a book Brian co-wrote with Jack Zeigler (the jacket photo shows Brian and Jack on the stoop of their brownstone on 78th street). Danny discovers that he can fly one day after missing out on playtime in the park with his friends because he had to do chores, then help a bunch of people, then get suckered into doing more work for a feckless kid. In his rush to get to the park as daylight wanes he nearly falls down a steep street. As he flaps his arms to keep from falling he starts to go up and up. Soon he is flying around the town, to his and everybody's amazement. Danny gets co-opted by a greedy carnival man who wants to exploit his ability for the almighty dollar. Danny can't perform under such circumstances. It seems that only in doing nice things for other people can Danny gain the ability to transcend gravity.

It's a lovely book and a good message for our (and any) kids. It is a quirky member of our kids' library. One could probably say the same for Brian—a quirky and lovely, good person for all of us. Life has added distance between my family and the McConnachies over the years but they are the type that would be easy to reconnect with probably at any point, such is the density of our shared experience in the 1970s-2000s in NYC, and the easy warmth of Brian's personality. I can remember his voice from an NPR piece maybe 7 years ago—he sounded the same then as I remember him from decades ago. Kind, approachable, wise, inquisitive, with a glint of the whimsical and fantastic, sort of like a flying boy.

Oh, I forgot to mention his inscription to me in my copy of *Flying Boy*.

"To Sam: Don't try it at night."

CHRIS KELLY

There are perfectly good books about the importance of Doug Kenney (by Josh Karp) and Michael O'Donoghue (by Dennis Perrin) and two about Tony Hendra (by Tony Hendra) but none about Brian McConnachie, who's at least as influential as they are. I wonder why that is.

I suppose he missed the boat by not being dead or Tony Hendra.

I remember Brian being more, uhm, inner-directed than some of the other editors. There was no trail of broken glass, hurt feelings and Class 2 drug crimes. When I was a tween, underfoot at the *Lampoon*, my main impression of Brian McConnachie was that he was Henry Beard.

It was only later, when I learned to read (sophomore year, college), that I discovered that Brian McConnachie was screamingly funny. For instance:

EMMA PEELE CONTEST
That's right, Miss Emma Peele, the one and only, will, for an unspecified period of time, smash you from pillar to post. Heedless of your pitiful cries for mercy, our Miss Peele will kick, punch, jab, chop, and God only knows what else at your cowering, panting body. Just when you think she's tiring and willing to relent, she offers you her hand and you go to accept it and then whammo —her knee right in your groin. And that's not all. Directly following your beating, you will be rushed by private car to the fabulous Cedars of Lebanon Hospital—hospital to the stars. There you will spend one whole week of carefree recovery as your memory conjures up the most vivid recollections of Miss Emma Peele: her cat-like crouch, her svelte spring, the aroma from her auburn hair filling your nostrils that second before she flung you to the far wall. No, no, they can't take that away from you. During your stay at Cedars, you will enjoy around-the-clock nurses. And here comes one now to take your temperature. Isn't that nice? But wait, why, that's no nurse! It's Emma Peele sneaking in to disconnect your IV and break a chair over your chest.

Brian McConnachie is one of those rare comic writers who's so funny he makes you yourself less funny, as you force other people to read him while you watch. Like I did, to you, just now.

The other explanation for the lack of a Brian McConnachie cult is that his work is almost impossible to categorize, much less explain. How do you recommend him to someone? Who could you possibly say he was like?

Is the Emma Peele Contest a parody? If so, of what? Robert Motherwell said that abstract expressionism resists interpretation. It's like that. Only with Diana Rigg beating you up.

But why? And where could an idea like that start?

One possible clue: In 1971, Diana Rigg appeared fleetingly naked in Ronald Millar's play *Abelard and Heloise*, and McConnachie slipped quietly away from the *Lampoon* offices—as was his wont—and saw it again and again and again.

By some accounts, "again and again and again and again."

Around our house it was believed he also carried field glasses and always sat in the front row.

Or maybe I'm thinking of Henry Beard.

Another clue: A strange man appears at the end of Brian McConnachie and Francis Hollidge's comic, "Heading for Trouble." He announces, like it explains anything: "The world we live in is no joke." This man is never identified, but I think he's supposed to be Dana Andrews. So "Heading for Trouble," which is one of the three funniest things in the world, might be about Dana Andrews. But why?

Your guess is as good as mine.

ORRIN GROSSMAN

I have known Brian since 1979, when we were members of a New York City Upper West Side babysitting co-op. The idea was, you would exchange babysitting services with other new parents, thus avoiding excessive charges from rapacious teenagers then dominating the babysitting market in a wilder, grittier New York City. Surprisingly quickly the other parents stopped requesting my and Brian's services and we were left with a number of chits which we passed back and forth between ourselves. Soon we were strolling in Central and Riverside Park with Mary and Erica, who are now in their forties and apparently none the worse.

Thus began a 40-year friendship that has enriched my life in many ways, none of them financial. Of course, Brian is a great storyteller; this is true whether recounting sanitized stories from *SCTV* and *SNL*, or from his own colorful family. Few people have as rich a collection of anecdotes exploring the highways and byways of the human heart.

And I will forever be in his debt for getting me into the Harvard Club of NYC. During my college years my social skills had not yet advanced to the ability to form friendships, so I knew nobody at the Club who could sponsor me—but Brian did. How many of us can boast of friendships that range from John Belushi to Governor George Pataki? Surely that speaks to a quality of empathy and openness worth emulating. Or perhaps a lack of principles.

Now that Brian has moved to Florida I must rely on the phone instead of the drives to Garrison I enjoyed so much. I have not forgiven him for this move, but I still love him. His voice, his humor, his love of the odd, the eccentric, the slightly off comment, remains as strong as ever, and I look forward to many years of enjoying his company.

DENNIS PERRIN

Brian is the plainest genius I've known. I've known a few geniuses, mostly by accident, and usually they felt the need to jazz it up, to reinforce what made them special.

Not Brian.

Anyone who knows him knows what I'm talking about. So this goes straight to Brian:

I love you. You have long inspired me, though I can't touch your creative output. If I could, you'd be writing about me. Well, maybe if Mike talked you into it.

I love the idea that those you currently know have little idea of who you really are, or what you've done. One of America's greatest humorists is hiding in plain sight, which, given your brilliance, is perfect.

SEAN KELLY

Brian's office at the *Lampoon* was across the hall from mine. His had a window (overlooking Madison Avenue). Occasionally he would put a big-ish sign in his window for the entertainment of the civilians who toiled in the building across the street.

"SMILE IF YOU'RE NOT WEARING UNDERWEAR"

One evening Brian loomed in my open door. His glasses, as usual, flickered with an extraterrestrial twinkle.

"Sean, can I get your opinion about something?"

"Sure. Come in. Sit."

"Well, I'm trying to write a comic about those annoying Dana Andrews TV commercials against drunk driving."

"Of course you are."

"So far, I have Mister Peanut and the Pillsbury Doughboy in a convertible and they're both clearly plastered and weaving all over the highway—"

"Who's driving?"

"Mister Peanut."

"That makes sense."

"And Mister Peanut is shouting something to the Doughboy, something about his aunt."

"Brian, I'm not sure I'm following…"

"He yells at him, 'Your aunt, you know, the one with the small feet.'"

[*A pause.*]

"What I can't decide is, would 'small hands' be funnier? What do you think?"

THE CURTAIN IS LOWERED TO INDICATE THE PASSAGE OF FORTY YEARS

Brian and I have agreed to answer questions from the audience after a screening of the *Lampoon* documentary. This enterprise, under any circumstances, is one part narcissism and two parts masochism. It's especially excruciating when one is expected to provide witty ripostes.

We've agreed that Brian will field the third and final question. It turns out to be a long and complicated one and—I think—slightly hostile: something about satire and the zeitgeist.

Brian appears to give the matter much consideration. His glasses glitter dangerously. At length, he elucidates, "Suppose you owned a pretty little roadside café, but bikers kept showing up and scaring the other customers off."

[*A pause.*]

"The thing to do would be to hang many flowerpots full of geraniums from the porch roof. I think that'd do the trick."

DEBORAH McMANUS

Glasses (no, not those reading things with strings!) raised and hats off to Brian McConnachie, a funny, gentle and kind man, neighbor, excellent dancer and lovely friend for 41 years for God's sake. Our kids grew up together and Brian and Ann and Jason and I just plain grew together. It was a sweet time with caroling, swimming after fierce tennis games, dinners and too much vodka (sigh). Oh my—were we not lucky!!!

A limited edition of 25 Giclée prints on archival stock, 8" x 10", signed by R. O. Blechman and Nicholas Blechman, is available for $325, postage included. Inquire at ro@roblechman.com.

They'll go fast!

NOTES FROM A SMALL PLANET

The love that dare not meow its name • ***By Rick Geary***

EVERY THING WENT WRONG
RICK GEARY ©17
I SPENT AN AFTERNOON RECENTLY AT THE HOME OF MY FRIEND NATE.
ALL WENT WELL UNTIL WE STARTED ARGUING POLITICS.
ON ANY OTHER SUBJECT HE IS USUALLY QUITE RATIONAL.
FINALLY, I FOUND IT NECESSARY TO BRAIN HIM WITH A TABLE LEG.
I'M SURE I LEFT FINGERPRINTS ALL OVER.
AS WELL AS TRACKS FROM MY DISTINCTIVE SNEAKERS.
BUS
IN MY AGITATED STATE, I BOARDED THE WRONG BUS...
WHICH DEPOSITED ME IN A FAR CORNER OF TOWN.
I PAUSED ON A BRIDGE TO DISPOSE OF MY SHOES AND THE TABLE LEG.
BUT AN ANGRY GUY STARTED YELLING AT ME ABOUT DUMPING TRASH IN THE RIVER.
I RAN FROM HIM AS FAST AS I COULD.
THEN THE CLOUDS BURST!
AS I RAN, I BEGAN COMPILING A MENTAL LIST...
OF ALL THE FOOLISH AND HEEDLESS THINGS I'VE DONE IN MY LIFE.
12
SUFFICE IT TO SAY I WAS LATE GETTING HOME.

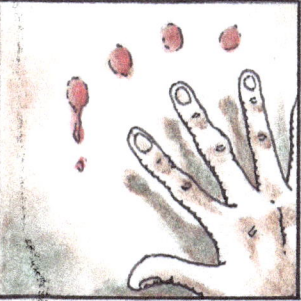

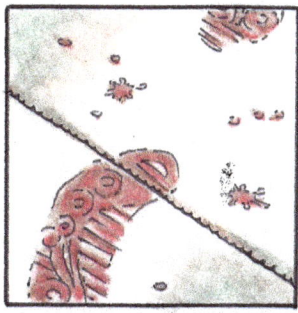

THE KRONINGER COLLECTION
Treasures from one man's fabulous stash of pop culture ephemera. • By Stephen Kroninger

KEY: **1** Martin & Lewis *Money From Home* lenticular (1953), The Paul Hesse Studio, made by Harvey Prever. This was a wedding anniversary present from my wife. **2** Concord Stompers button. From the garbage route I worked on in my youth. **3** *Garbage Pail Kids* pin (c.1986). Prototype that never went into production. **4** Henny Youngman wooden nickel **5** Glenn Strange as the Frankenstein monster: "Monstrous" blacklight poster, 1973. Hung over my teenage bed, now on my studio door. **6** *Mo' Better Blues* badge (1990) signed by Spike Lee. **7** Ghost Viewer for William Castle's *13*

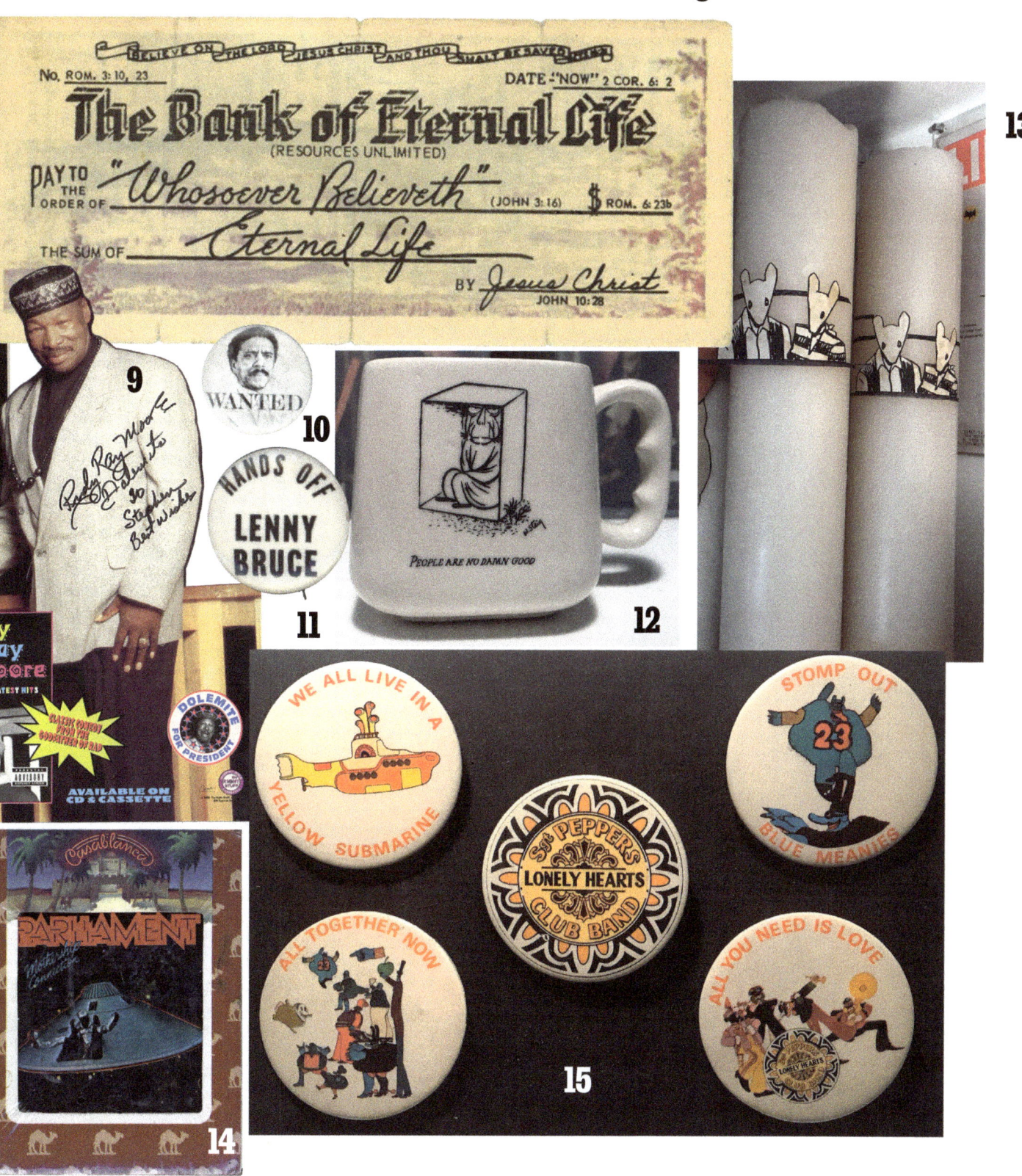

Ghosts (1960). **8** Bank of Eternal Life check signed by Jesus Christ; another pickup on the garbage route. **9** Signed Rudy Ray Moore cardboard standup (1995). **10** Richard Pryor *Wanted* button (1978). **11** "Hands Off Lenny Bruce" button (c. 1960s). **12** William Steig mug **13** Centerpiece candles from the wedding reception of Art Spiegelman & Francoise Mouly. **14** Parliament *Mothership Connection* 8-track. Sealed. **15** Complete set of Beatles *Yellow Submarine* buttons (1968). A complete set is rare; they didn't sell well, and most were destroyed by the manufacturer. ***NOTE:*** *Items are not to scale.* **B**

LAST LOOK?

Donald Trump by **ZOE MATTHIESSEN**

www.ingramcontent.com/pod-product-compliance
Lightning Source LLC
Chambersburg PA
CBHW061755290426
44108CB00029B/3002